Insight Publishing Company
Sevierville, Tennessee

Published by Insight Publishing Company
P.O. Box 4189
Sevierville, Tennessee 37864

Printed in the United States of America

ISBN: 1-885640-27-7

Table Of Contents

A Message From The Publisher

Some of my most rewarding experiences in business, and for that matter in my personal life, have been at meetings, conventions, or gatherings after the formal events have concluded. Inevitably, small groups of ten to fifteen men and women gather together to rehash the happenings of the day and to exchange war stories, recently heard jokes, or the latest gossip from their industry. It is in these informal gatherings where some of the best lessons can be learned.

Usually, in informal groups of professionals, there are those who clearly have lived through more battles and learned more lessons than the others. These are the men and women who are really getting the job done and everyone around the room knows it. When they comment on the topic of the moment, they don't just spout the latest hot theory or trend, and they don't ramble on and on without a relevant point. These battle scarred warriors have lessons to share that everyone senses are just a little more real, more relevant, and therefore worthy of more attention.

These are the kind of people we have recruited to offer their insights and expertise for *Conversations On Success*. The book is filled with frank and powerful discussions with men and women who are making a significant impact on their culture, in their field, and on their colleagues and clients. It is ripe with "the good stuff," as an old friend of mine used to always say. Inside these pages you'll find ideas, insights, strategies, and philosophies that are working with real people, in real companies, and under real circumstances.

It is our hope that you keep this book with you until you've dog-eared every chapter and made so many notes in the margins that you have trouble seeing the original words on the pages. There is treasure here. Enjoy digging!

Interviews conducted by:

David E. Wright
President, International Speakers Network

Chapter 1

LES BROWN

THE INTERVIEW

David E. Wright (Wright)

Today we're talking to Les Brown, an internationally recognized speaker and CEO of Les Brown Enterprises, Inc. He is also the author of the highly acclaimed and successful books, *Live Your Dreams* and the newly released book, *It's Not Over Until You Win*. Les is the former host of the *Les Brown Show,* a nationally syndicated daily television talk show which focused on solutions rather than problems. Les Brown is one of the nation's leading authorities in understanding and stimulating human potential. Utilizing powerful delivery and newly emerging insights, Les's customized presentations will teach, inspire, and channel any audience to new levels of achievement. Les Brown, welcome to *Conversations on Success.*

Les Brown (Brown)

Thank you very much. It's a pleasure to be here.

Wright

Les, you've been a role model for thousands of people down through the years because of your triumph over adversity. Tell our readers a little bit about your early life and who was responsible for your rearing.

Brown

Well, I was born in a poor section of Miami, Florida called Liberty City. I was born in an abandoned building on a floor with a twin brother. When we were six weeks of age, we were adopted. In the fifth grade, I was identified as EMR (Educable Mental Retarded) and put back into the fourth grade. I failed again when I was in the eighth grade. I attribute everything that I've done to my mother. I always quote Abraham Lincoln when I give a presentation, "All that I am and all that I ever hope to be I owe to my mother." I saw a sign once that said, "God took me out of my biological mother's womb and placed me in the heart of my adopted mother." I love my adopted mother's faith, her character, her drive, her dedication, and her willingness to do whatever it took to raise seven children by herself. She only had a third grade education but she had a Ph.D. in mothering.

Wright

If I remember correctly, you were diagnosed at the age of 36 with dyslexia. How did that happen?

Brown

No, no, not dyslexia. I was never diagnosed with dyslexia. I was in special education from fourth grade all the way through senior high school. My education ended at that time in the formal sense, but I became very much interested in personal development tapes and books because of a high school teacher who challenged me to do something in a class and I told him I couldn't do it and he insisted that I could. Finally, I said, "I can't because I'm Educable Mentally Retarded." He said, "Don't ever say that again. Someone's opinion of you does not have to become your reality." His name was Mr. Leroy Washington, he's still around today. One of the things that he emphasized to all of his students was that you don't get in life what you want, you get in life what you are. What you achieve, what you produce in life, is a reflection of your growth and development as a person. So, you must invest in yourself. He often quoted scripture by saying, "Be ye not conformed to this world, be ye transformed by the renewing of your mind." He said most people fail in life because they don't know that they don't know and they think they know. They suffer from mental malnutrition. He said if you take the time each day to develop your mind, read ten to fifteen pages of something positive every day, find some goals that are beyond your comfort zone that can challenge you to reinvent yourself because in order to do something you've never done you've got to be someone you've never been. He said the possibilities of what you could achieve by developing your mind and developing your communication skills—because once you open your mouth you tell the world who you are—you can really begin to climb the ladder of success and do things that will literally amaze you.

Wright

So, your education is self-education.

Brown

Yes.

Wright

Listening to tapes and reading books and that sort of thing?

Brown

Yes. Going to seminars and then testing and experimenting. I think it's very important that people experiment with their lives and find out what it is that works for them, what gives their lives a sense of joy and meaning. What is it that brings music to your life? That way you're able to discover some talents, abilities, and skills that you don't even realize that you have.

Wright

I remember reading your first book, *Live Your Dreams*. This best seller is helping people even today. Can you tell us what you're trying to say in this book and why it is important?

Brown

What I'm doing in *Live Your Dreams* is challenging people to look at their situation and ask themselves some crucial questions. Is life working for me? Is it really giving me what I want? When most people get out of high school, they end up doing things that other people want them to do. I think it was Albert Schweitzer who was asked a question, "What's wrong with humankind today?" He said, "Men simply don't think." He said that in a generic sense. Men and women simply don't challenge themselves to think about what it is that really makes them happy and gives their life a sense of meaning, purpose, power and value. So, challenge people to think about what it is that really gives their life a sense of meaning and power. Once you determine that, assess yourself. What are your strengths? What are your weaknesses? What is it you bring to the table of life? What help? What assistance? What training? What education? What resources? What do you have to tap into that will help you to become the kind of person that can produce those results? Then next is commit yourself. Don't ask yourself how am I going to do it. How is none of your business. What is most important is to get started. The how will come. The way will come. Everything you need to attract, the people, the resources, the assistance, will come to be available at your disposal.

Wright

What do you think about goal setting? There has been so much written about it lately.

Brown

I think it's very important that people set goals because what it does is allow you to focus your energy. It helps you to put together a game plan and a strategy and an agenda for your life. If you don't have an agenda for your life, then you're going to be a part of somebody else's agenda. Therefore, you want to set some goals. There's a quote I love very much that says, "People who aim at nothing in life usually hit nothing dead on the head."

Wright

Oh, my.

Brown

Yes, so you want to have some goals that you are setting in each area of your life. You want to monitor those goals after you put together a plan of action to achieve those goals. You break those goals down into manageable increments. You want to have long range and short range goals, three month goals, thirty day goals, and weekly goals, daily tasks and activities that you engage in that will move you in the direction of your goals. Robert Schuller said something that is true, he said, "By the yard it's hard, but inch by inch anything is a cinch." As you begin to look at the big picture and come back to where you are right now, looking at the big picture completed of where you want to go, then you begin to put together a strategy of things and activities you need to do each day to move you in the direction of those goals. As you get closer to those goals that you have set for yourself in the various areas of your life, your physical life, your emotional life, your spiritual life, your financial life, then you begin to push the goals back. Continue to stretch, continue to push yourself, and reach further.

Wright

A few years ago you had a nationally syndicated television talk show. It's next to impossible to get a show of that nature on the air. Tell us the circumstances that helped your successful efforts to get your show on the air.

Brown

Well, and I believe I'm coming back, I don't think it's impossible to get back on again. What I did was, I wanted to go in a different direction—television in the time that I ventured into it was based upon a formula that they were accustomed to that they'd always implemented which was the show must be based upon conflict and controversy. So, you had Phil Donahue, Oprah Winfrey, Sally Jesse Raphael and Geraldo. My show was based upon solutions. I felt that you could have a show that was not based upon conflict and controversy. That you could have a show where you would look at what the challenges are that people are facing. Who is it that has gone through it and is on the other side of the challenge? Talk to that person and find out how they got there. Interview a guest that's in the middle of it and find one that's just approaching that challenge. Have an expert work them through that process over the hour, asking what is it that brought you here? There's an old saying that wherever you find yourself, at some point and time you made an appointment to get there. The other thing is that success leaves clues. What we must do is talk to someone who's had the same problem that you've had and find out from their experience what is it that you can do to implement a game plan. What help and support will you need to work through this problem? It was very successful. It was the highest rated and fastest cancelled talk show in the history of television. Because, even though it had successful ratings, the producers of the show wanted me to do a show based upon conflict and controversy and sensationalism—fathers who sleep with their 14 year old daughter's boyfriends. I decided to be true to my concept and not venture off into those other areas and do those Jerry Springer type shows and they cancelled the show and brought someone else in who was willing to cooperate with what they wanted.

Wright

Did you learn any lessons from your highly competitive talk show?

Brown

Yes. The lesson that I learned was that I should have been the executive producer. I was hired talent, therefore, the hand that pays the piper calls the tune. Had I been the executive producer of my show like Oprah Winfrey, then I could have done what Oprah did after she saw the success of my show, she changed directions and used the formula that we'd come up with and then the rest is history. I would've put my own production company together, continued to do the show that I was doing, and would've found someone else to syndicate the show nationally and if not nationally I would've set it up to do it locally and then rolled it back out nationally myself if I had it to do over again.

Wright

I bet you still get stopped on the street with people who watched your commercials on PBS station for many years. Those were some of the best produced I've ever seen.

Brown

Well, thank you. We've gotten a lot of response from PBS. We just did one show four months ago called, *It's in Your Hands* on PBS. In fact, I end the show with my children because five of my seven children are speakers as well and trainers. What we're doing is teaching people how to become responsible for their careers, their health, and for their family life. The response has been very, very successful on PBS.

Wright

So, you're growing your own speakers, then.

Brown

Yes, I'm training speakers. I'm more of a speech coach. I've developed a reputation as a speaker, but I have a gift in helping people to tell their story and to position it so it has value for an audience. Have it create special, magical moments within the context of their presentation so that it can create a committed listening with an audience and move them to new heights within themselves.

Wright

Yeah, you don't have to tell me that you're a sought after speaker. We were planning a speaking engagement in Ohio and the two people that they wanted more than any were Stephen Covey and Les Brown. They really came after you, so you do have quite a reputation for helping people.

Brown

Thank you.

Wright

A lot of our readers have read many books that advocate focus in their career. I know you've done several things and you've done them well. Also, you've been successful doing many things. Do you advocate going in one direction and not diversifying in your career?

Brown

I think that you have to find one area that you want to focus on and as you develop momentum in that area and reach a certain measure of success, then you can branch off into other areas.

Wright

Les, you had a serious bought with cancer a few years ago.

Brown

Yes.

Wright

How did this catastrophic disease effect your life?

Brown

What cancer did for me was it helped me to live life with a sense of urgency that tomorrow is not guaranteed. It helped me to begin to reprioritize my life where you begin to ask the question what's really important. Then you spend more time focusing on those things. So, even though I really always practiced and advocated that people live each day as if it were their last, it helps you to begin to focus even more so. That's what I began to be about the business of doing, think-

7

ing about my legacy, spending more time with my children, my grandchildren, and friends that I cared about, and working on the purpose that I've embraced for my life.

Wright

My wife was going through cancer at the same time you were, I remember. I heard her say recently that even though she doesn't want cancer again, she wouldn't give anything for the lessons that she learned going through it.

Brown

Yes. It helps, it gives new meaning to life and you value things that you used to take for granted.

Wright

So, you did gain a lot of insight into what's important?

Brown

Oh, without any question I did.

Wright

Your new book, *It's Not Over Until You Win*, has been long awaited, of course. Would you tell our readers what it's about and what you're trying to say?

Brown

I think that what people must do is challenge themselves to overcome the inner conversation that has been placed in us through our conditioning, through our environment and our circumstances because we live in a world that we're told more about our limitations rather than our potential. To overcome and to defeat that conversation that tells you can't do something. Most people, if you ask them, if they have ever been told that they can't achieve a goal that they envision for their self will say, "yes." Most people when they think about something they want to do focus more on what it is that they don't have going for them as opposed to the things that they have going for them. My whole goal is to help people to learn how to become unstoppable. Yes, it's going to be difficult. It's going to be hard. You're going to have obstacles thrown in your path. You will have set backs and disappointments. But, you must develop the mindset of a winner. You must come back again and again and again. You must be creative and flexible. You must be versatile and adaptable and never stop until you reach your goals.

Wright

I read many years ago that 98 percent of all failure comes from quitting. Would you agree with that?

Brown

Without any question. Most people become discouraged and they see a delay as a denial. I encourage people to go back to the drawing board of their minds, regroup, get some other fresh thinking. Einstein said, "The thinking that has brought me this far has created some problems that this thinking can't solve." Sometimes we have to begin to allow other people to be a part of the process, to look at the situation that we're battling with new eyes that can help us to overcome the challenges that we're facing.

Wright

As I have said before, you have been a role model for thousands of adults as well as young people. Do you have any advice to give our readers that would help them to grow in body, mind, and spirit and live a better, fuller life?

Brown

Yes. I think it's important that people raise the bar on themselves everyday. Look at your life and understand and know that you are greater than you give yourself credit for being, you have talents and abilities that you haven't even begun to reach for yet. Jim Ron has a quote I love, he says, "When the end comes for you, let it find you conquering a new mountain, not sliding down an old one." So, therefore, we have to raise the bar on ourselves constantly and assess ourselves. The other thing is that I believe that it's important that we ask for help, not because we're weak but because we want to remain strong. Many people don't ask for help because of pride. Pride cometh before a fall because of ego. Ego means edging God out. Ask for help, not because you're weak but because you want to remain strong. I think that you also have to ask yourself, what is your plan for being here? Most people take their health for granted, that living a long, healthy life is not a given. Pain is a given. But being here, you have to fight to stay here. You have to have a plan of action to stay here. So, what is your plan for being here? Put yourself on your to do list. Develop a plan of action on how you're going to take better care of your-self and spend more time with people that you care about and focus on living the goals and dreams that you've envisioned for yourself that's the calling on your life.

Wright

Down through the years, as you've made your decisions, has faith played an important role in your life?

Brown

Yes. Faith is very important. I think that you have to believe in yourself, believe in your abilities, believe in your dreams, and believe in a power greater than yourself. There's a quote I love, it says, "Faith is the oil that takes the friction out of living." Do the best you can and leave the rest to a power greater than you.

Wright

Les, you don't know how much I appreciate you being with us to-day on *Conversations on Success*.

Brown

Oh, thank you so much.

Wright

Today we've been talking to Les Brown, an internationally recog-nized speaker and CEO of Les Brown Enterprises. He's the author of *Live Your Dreams* and *It's Not Over Until You Win*. I suggest that you run down to the bookstore and look for both of them. Les has been a successful talk show host and as we have heard today, he is now coaching speakers. Thank you so much for being with us, Les.

Brown

Thank you, I appreciate it very much.

About The Author

Les Brown is an internationally recognized speaker and CEO of Les Brown Enterprises, Inc. He is also the author of the highly acclaimed and successful books, *Live Your Dreams* and *It's Not Over Until You Win*. Les Brown is one of the nation's leading authorities in understanding and stimulating human potential.

Les Brown
Les Brown Enterprises
PO Box 27380
Detroit, Michigan 48227
Phone: 800.733.4226
Email: speak@lesbrown.com
Website: www.lesbrown.com

Chapter 2

RJ JACKSON

THE INTERVIEW

David E. Wright (Wright)

Today we're talking to Rita Jackson, known nationwide as *RJ*. She is not only a life skills intervention and prevention consultant, motivational speaker, radio personality and author, she is, indeed, a *"woman with a passion for people."* Undeterred by a rare eye disease, this gifted visionary shares her passion and personal challenges as well as offers powerful and practical life skill tips to enhance the lives of youth and women. As a pioneer in the field of personal development, RJ is serious about empowering teen girls and women and exposing them to the life skills necessary for success. Her passion for people and her commitment to serve has earned her numerous awards, including the Visionary of the Year Award, presented by the African-American Employees Association; the TURN (Tobacco Use Reduction Now) Volunteer of the Year Award, presented by the California State Health Department; Phenomenal Women of the Year Award 2002, presented by Professional Women in Business of America; and a certificate of recognition from the City of Richmond, Virginia in recognition of service and contributions made to empower women and teen girls. The Buffalo City Council declared June 24th Rita Jackson Day in the city of Buffalo. The mayor of Wickliffe, Ohio also honored RJ for her exceptional efforts to motivate and inspire women and teen girls. Turning Point Communications Magazine and Riverside Business Press Magazine recognized her extraordinary passion for community service and presented RJ with The 2003 Living History Maker in Education Award and The Leader of Distinction 2003 Award. RJ, welcome to *Conversations on Success.*

RJ Jackson (Jackson)

Hello David. Thank you for inviting me to share my passion for people.

Wright

When you say you have a passion for people, what does that mean? What has that passion driven you to do?

Jackson

Passion is a word that so many people use for so many things. It's almost become a meaningless word. When I say I have a passion for people I mean I have a love for people. I love people, not for what they can do for me, but simply because of who they are. I have a devotion for people to give my best to people. I have a commitment to people not only to give them my best, but help them become the best that they can be. That's what I mean when I say I have a passion for people.

It's funny that you ask what my passion has "driven" me to do. There was a time I really wanted a BMW. I knew the exact style, color and make. I remember driving to church and seeing the very car I envisioned. I took it for a test drive. I loved it! I told the car dealer to give me time to think about it. He tried to pressure me into buying it that minute. I didn't. The next day, I went to an office building where a friend of mine worked. I thought—this would be the perfect place to provide programs for teen girls and women. Instead of buying that BMW I used the one thousand dollars to sign a contract for an office suite where I provide free support groups for teen girls, single parents, and women. That is what my passion has driven me to do. Whenever people come to my office they have to take the elevator to the second floor. When they step off I always ask them, "How did you like the ride in my BMW."

Wright

Give an example of when your passion for people allowed you to make the difference between life and death for someone.

Jackson

I remember I had a very busy morning. I took my son to school, ran several errands, checked my e-mail and then sat down to listen to my voicemail. I heard a message from a woman. She didn't say much except, "RJ could you please call me" and then she left her phone number. I immediately called the woman back. I said, "This is RJ how can I help you?" She just started rambling. She said I never met her but she heard me speak at a breakfast event and that I encouraged her heart. Finally, she said, "I know I'm not making any sense, but I had these pain pills and I was just about to take them and the phone rang and it was you. I can't believe that you called me back, but you called just when I was going to end my life." She said that she got the phone book to search under the category of movie instead he eyes fell motivational speaker Rita Jackson. I didn't even know that my phone number was in the phone book. I later learned that she found me at the most desperate time of her life. Her oldest son had a heart attack and died. He was 26. Within a couple of weeks her second oldest son was brutally murdered. That morning she was reading the autopsy report. She was devastated. I prayed with her and talked with her and I invited her to come to a seminar that I was having. She was the first person to show up. Today, she has her own ministry called *Somebody Say Something*. It's a support group for people who witness a crime and are too afraid to get involved.

Wright

I've known some great platform speakers down through the last two or three decades. The great ones always tell me that they try to leave something behind for the people. One fellow, a psychiatrist out in California, calls them "take-a-ways." Could you name two or three things that you try to leave with people when you speak? What pieces of you do you try to leave behind?

Jackson

I always try to leave my eyes and my heart. In the natural, I cannot see you with my eyes because I have a rare eye condition called Kardaconis that causes me to have no focus in my eyes. Literally, you would consider me legally blind with the exception that I wear contacts that are specially created to give me vision. Most people only see with their natural eyes—I don't. I look at people with my heart. My heart does not see you as you are, but for what you can become. Can you imagine if everybody looked at people for what they could become instead of what they are? Can you imagine if mothers would look at teenagers lying on the couch watching TV and say, "Yep, that's a doctor right there or that's a computer technician." But most mothers might say, "That's one lazy child!" I want to leave my heart so other people can learn to see people with their hearts and not with their eyes.

My heart allows me to see the greatness in everyone. As I speak and share with other people, that is what I desire and encourage them to do—see the goodness in everyone in spite of who they are. Everyone has something to offer; everyone has a purpose in life.

Wright

What is the fingerprint that you are trying to leave on the lives of people that you have touched?

Jackson

It's called legacy. I simply want to leave a legacy of life. All I do is for the purpose of imparting life. For me, life is really not measured by what you have however; it is measured by what you give. When I say, "impart life" I mean to give hope where people feel hopeless. I mean to give love when people feel unloved or give encouragement when people feel discouraged.

Wright

What did you do and what were you thinking when 9-11 happened and the Twin Towers were falling down?

Jackson

Wow, 9-11. Life changing. Such an emotional day. I'm sure many people relived the feeling of 9-11 just recently with the New York power outage. On that day, 9-11, I remember preparing to take my son to school when my phone rang. It was my neighbor she said we were at war. She was just frantic and I was wondering, "What she was talking about. She said, "Turn your television on." I turned the television on and, like most Americans, spent half my day there thinking "Oh, my goodness." The only thing I could really do was pray for our country especially the families who were searching for their loved ones. I got down on my knees on the right side of my bed and just prayed and I cried and I prayed some more. In between praying and crying I was glued to the television. I remember calling people because I'm from New York and a lot of my family is still in New York. The one thing that really impressed me was how people were just reaching out—color, religion, neighborhoods, none of those factors were important any more. Today I am concerned about where that loving nature went. What happened to that kindness and that helping hand that we were all lending to each other on 9-11?

Wright

When you hear people say the word "accountability," what does that mean to you?

Jackson

Two words come to mind when I think of accountability. Number one is responsibility, because when you're held accountable that means you have to be responsible. You have a responsibility and that means that people are depending on you to do what you say you are going to do. When it comes to being responsible, you have something that other people need that makes this puzzle of life complete. Accountability and responsibility go hand in hand. Our first responsibility in life is to God. Then we have a responsibility to others as well as ourselves. Now days, people don't want to be responsible and they like blaming other people. We can look at television and see how often on talk shows people are saying, "It's my mother's fault or my father or my girlfriend, etc." We have to learn to be responsible, and when we learn more we have to become responsible to do more.

The other word that comes to mind when I think of accountability is a simple word—price. When you talk about accountability there is a price to pay. I'm reminded how we shop in the stores and look for discounts. Now, at a store when something is marked down because the box is damaged but there is nothing wrong with the product, we like that.

Wright

You've been watching me shop, haven't you?

Jackson

Well that's how I shop too. We all like to receive a discount. We all want a bargain. But with accountability there is a price to pay. Unfortunately, that's how we are with accountability. We want somebody to cut some slack for us. We don't want to pay the price or work as hard. Unfortunately, because we aren't willing to pay the price, the results that we're looking for aren't there. I feel a lot of people want something out of life, but they're not willing to pay the price. They aren't willing to be responsible to God, others or to themselves. When it comes to accountability, we have to be willing to be men and women of our word. Something as simple as saying, "Sure, I'll be at your event." Then the next day when it's time to go and you are too tired to go you say, "I'm just too tired." We've got to be willing to stick to our word because people have prepared for what we've said. If we say we're going to be there, they count that as a plate or a seat. They spend money and time preparing for us. So, accountability for me means responsibility and keeping your word—being willing to pay the price.

Wright

What are the keys to living a successful life?

Jackson

The keys for a successful life depend on what you define as success. For me, the first key is to realize that without God there is no success. Once you have God in your life, the keys that I go by that make my life happy everyday are: purpose and passion. Knowing your purpose—what you were created for—and then fulfilling your passion. You have a purpose in life. That purpose, whatever it is—to sing, speak, or dance—you have a purpose. Yet people aren't willing sometimes to discover what their purpose is.

Wright

In general, what would you say are the obstacles that cripple people and stop them from reaching their full potential?

Jackson

When I think of obstacles, I think of barriers—for instance, frustration. Frustration is simply a barrier that keeps us from getting what we want. We allow it to get in the way. If I can break down *obstacle* for you using several of the letters to answer your question, this is what I think. The **O** is for the *Opinions* of others that keep people from fulfilling their purposes in life. We allow other people to kill our dreams. They will say to us, "Well, how do you think you're going to do that?" And we believe we can't do something just based on what they say, their opinion. The **B** in obstacle stands for *Believing* that your goals are unreachable. That's another obstacle that keeps us from being successful. When you believe that your goals are reachable, guess what, they are. But when you believe that they are not reachable, guess what, they're not. The **S** is *Staying* in one place for too long. That keeps us from fulfilling our purpose. In my opinion, expansion is one of the keys that unlock success—reaching out and going out, forming relationships with people and doing things, that's when we become successful. So, when we're in a job, we can't just stay there because it pays the bills, we've got to be somewhere that's going to bring up our contentment level as well. But many people do that. They go to work everyday and stay there because it pays the bills. So, staying somewhere too long can be an obstacle. Another obstacle is **T**reating people badly or with disrespect. You cannot reach your potential if you are not willing to treat people with respect. The same way you treat them is the same way you're going to be treated. If you want something you've go to give something. I'm reminded of what Zig Zigler says, "You can have anything in life you want if you're just willing to treat other people the way you want to be treated." Then as I narrow this down, the **A** is for *Accepting* the fear over faith. That will keep you from reaching your potential. When you allow fear to rob you of the possibilities of reaching your potential you will not be successful in life. So, if you want to open up a business but you're scared, then that fear will keep you from opening up that business. The other thing we have to do, David, is *Care* more about what God says about our lives and other people. When we do not care about what God says it becomes an obstacle. How do we reach our full potential? What are the obstacles that keep us from doing that? When we **L**isten to the wrong people, then we fail to reach our potential. Listening is very important. I always say, "When you listen, you learn and learning is fun!" Listening is an art and it takes time. Unfortunately, most people do not want to take time to listen to people of wisdom. They want an answer quick, fast and in a hurry. If we want to reach our full potential, we must be willing to listen to wise people. People who have been where we desire to go, people who can help us get where we are going, and people who care to see us succeed in life. Listening to the wrong people will cause us to miss the mark. The final obstacle that keeps us from reaching our full potential is **E**xpecting to Fail. Have you ever caught yourself saying, "I can't do it, I'll never make it, or I would try it but I don't think that is for me?" If so, you are not alone. Most people have a desire to succeed but do not have the expectance it takes to succeed. The saying "What you think is what you get" is nothing but truth. If you expect to fail you will. If you expect to succeed and reach your full potential, you will. The question is what are you expecting?

Wright

What is your vision for women and the youth of America?

Jackson

My vision is very simple—that women and youth will change their roles as the number one consumers to the number one contributors of America. My hope is that women and youth will be recognized as people of integrity, influence, and impact. My vision is that people, particularly the women and youths, will not only make a difference but will be the difference. They will be women and teens of excellence, compassion, and responsibility. My vision is that they will be greater leaders loving life and living it to the fullest. It's a simple vision.

Wright

You have spoken before millions of people. Could you tell me about one face in the millions that you remember and how that meeting reminds you that your mission is being accomplished?

Jackson

I met a young lady that I had in one of my teen parenting programs. She was 17 years old and a teen mom of twins. Her twins were born premature and they were in the hospital for a while after they were born. She would come to school on the days that I presented to her school. When I wasn't there she wouldn't come. There came a day when she wasn't there. I was told that over the weekend one of her babies died. The funeral is today in about an hour. I had to go to this funeral. I ran home and I wrote out a check. I got to the funeral and heard someone asked if anybody wants to give words of encouragement. I went up. I gave them the check. Some time later I asked all of the students to write a letter about someone who encouraged or changed their life as a class project. This young lady wrote her letter to me about me. I carried that letter around with me. She left me a voicemail saying that the next day was her birthday and that there was nothing else in the world that she wanted to do but spend it with me. I arranged for her to spend the night with me and my daughters.

Earlier that same night I had to do a workshop. During the workshop I read her letter to the women in the workshop and I told them that today is her birthday. She was outside in the hallway. When she came in everybody stood up, sang happy birthday to her and gave her gifts and money. After the workshop I had a surprise birthday party for her. I don't know what they meant to her, but it meant the world to me. To answer your question David, out of all the millions of faces that I've seen, talked to and had the opportunity to bless, I'm always reminded of this young lady.

Wright

What a wonderful conversation. I want you to know how much I appreciate you spending this much time with me today. I really did learn a lot.

Jackson

David, before we go, there's one more thing I want you to know. If no one has said this to you today let me be the first to say—you are somebody special!

Wright

Today we have been talking to RJ, a woman with passion for people. Thank you so much, RJ, for being with us today.

Jackson

God bless you.

About The Author

Rita Jackson known nationwide as "RJ" is far more than a life skills consultant, motivational speaker, and author, she is indeed "A Woman with Passion for People." Undeterred by a rare eye disease, this gifted visionary and personal development pioneer enjoy sharing her passion, personal challenges, and shrewd strategies to enrich the quality of life. Her commitment to serve has earned her numerous awards. The city of Buffalo declared June 24 as "Rita "RJ" Jackson" Day.

RJ Jackson

PO Box 78

Bloomington, California 92316

Phone: 909.820.6066

Email: Ritajackson1.com

Website: www.ritajackson1.com

Chapter 3

DIANE DiRESTA

THE INTERVIEW

David E. Wright (Wright)

Today we are talking to Diane DiResta author of *Knockout Presentations, How To Deliver Your Message with Power, Punch, and Pizzazz.* She's more than just an author who likes to speak rather she's really a speaker who just happens to have written a book. As one of the leading presentation trainers in the country, Diane knows exactly what it takes to give a knockout presentation, and she is committed to helping others deliver them as well. With more than 15 years of experience in providing public speaking training for Fortune 500 Company executives, celebrities, and sports figures nationwide, Diane has build a solid expertise in helping a wide variety of high level professionals improve their communication skills and become more effective public speakers. As a knock out presenter herself, Diane has become a sought-after speaker, facilitator, and coach for some of today's largest businesses and organizations. Diane, welcome to *Conversations on Success.*

Diane DiResta (DiResta)

Thank you.

Wright

Diane, could you tell us a little bit about your background and how you came to enter the field of executive coaching?

DiResta

Well, I was originally clinically trained. I have a Masters Degree from Columbia in Speech Pathology, and I worked with children in the school system in New York City public schools. I really earned my stripes there. That was some of the best training I ever received. Then I made a career change, spent a short time with a consulting company, and then I did management training for the investment banking firms Salomon Brothers and Drexel Burnham. Then I went off on my own. I started to develop my own programs and here I am 12 years later.

Wright

So you choose to deal with executives now?

DiResta

I work with executives, with managers, and also employees on a seminar level.

Wright

Some of your satisfied clients are really impressive: AT&T, Chase Manhattan Bank, and IBM, just to name a few. As I understand it, you coach these companies using a three-part magic formula called Exec-U-Lead. Could you tell our readers a little bit about this formula?

DiResta

Exec-U-Lead is actually my executive coaching program. That's one program that I offer. The first process is to do an assessment. So I sit down with the individual and the executives and find out what it is that they want. Where are the gaps and where are they losing credibility or power in their communication. Then I design a program that's specific for them. So there is no one outline. Everybody's a little bit different and has different needs. Stage three is the follow up. *We really celebrate their wins* and we check in and we make sure that it's working for them, so that they can make sure they have a dramatic improvement in their skills, their performance, and their confidence. I also work one on one with people who are not executives. I was just working yesterday with a lawyer. I show people how to project their power.

Wright

I guess one of the most important parts of that tripod, if you will, is the follow up. Most of the consulting firms that I have been familiar with in the past don't really do a good job in the follow up, which is really, really important, isn't it?

DiResta

It's very important and I have to say many companies are not committed to that. If they were, they would really get better results in training. It's not enough to simply talk, give a motivational speech, or to train people for a couple of days. You need to come back and reinforce those skills. Companies that do make that investment, reap the benefits. They get the greatest return.

Wright

Right. In your book *Knockout Presentations, How To Deliver Your Message With Power, Punch, and Pizzazz*, you write about the ongoing debate over which is more important in a presentation, style or substance. Can you give us your opinion?

DiResta

Yes, they are both important, but I often have people debate this when I am speaking on the subject. Pretty much it's fifty-fifty. Some will say its substance; some will say its style. I say that what is most important is your delivery. Because, if you have good substance, you have good content and you can't deliver it in a way that gets attention and keeps attention, it doesn't matter what you have to offer. People won't get it. They won't listen and they won't stay long enough to hear your recommendation, your proposal, and the case that you have built. I assume that most people know their subject, because if you don't, you wouldn't even be there in the first place. However, substance is important too because there are some people who have great platform skills. But then you go away later after you've been pumped up and you have to think, "What did they really say?" There really wasn't any essence to the message, and there was nothing they could take away and use. So they are both very important. If you structure your message clearly or logically in terms of the listeners' point of view and then you deliver it with passion and with excitement, you'll be a knock out presenter. But I say that if I had to choose one, I would choose delivery because you have a very short amount of time to get someone's attention and people will turn off very quickly. Do you want me to give you an example?

Wright

Please.

DiResta

Okay. For an example, last night I went to hear a presentation. It was a sales seminar. It was two hours. It could have been 45 minutes to an hour because she dragged out the content. It was too slow. It was too basic. Her opening was good because she started by asking the audience questions. But then, she gave us some really basic reasons why you needed sales skills that we all know, and that should have been one sentence. People were disappointed in the presentation. She has a really good background and knowledge. Had she condensed that and thought about whom that audience was and delivered it with more passion and more excitement, she would have had a good talk.

Wright

You know I've been booking speakers, professional speakers, around the country now for 13 years. Being a part of the industry obviously one of the first things you learn is the greatest fear is the fear of public speaking, even greater than one's own death or loss of life, loss of limbs, or almost any other catastrophic thing that can happen to us. What I really enjoyed about your book and felt really good about was that you cover a wide range of reasons why that's true and give suggestions on how to get through those problems. I say that it is just to ask this question. When someone comes to you to help them conquer their fears of say nervousness, stage fright, what steps do you take them through?

DiResta

First let me say that I begin my talks by telling people that today more than ever their success depends on how well they present themselves and their message and their value. When you talk about *Conversations on Success*, this to me is one of the most important success skills, and people actually sabotage their success by avoiding public speaking. The first thing they need to do is to acknowledge that they have a fear and be willing to confront it. There are a number of things you can do. When I ask people in my surveys "Why are you afraid?" they give me lots of reasons but it all boils down to this. I think people are afraid of humiliation, the fear of being humiliated in public. When I've worked one on one with people who have a really strong fear, I can usually trace it back to some childhood incident where they were embarrassed in school or some situation. Part of getting over the fear is being able to develop the skill, because confidence comes with practice, with success.

So, when you do something, and you do it over and over again, and you learn the skills and you start to become better at it, you start to lose some of the fear. It's like driving. The first time you were all over the road and then after a while you can get to a place without even thinking about it. I work on a very simplistic skill level, and I talk about the science of speaking. I tell them this is what confidence looks like, this is what it sounds like, and this is the language of confidence. They know what it is. It's not a nebulous, ambiguous process. I give them the actual formulas and skills. Then, I work with them on one skill at a time because it's over whelming to be up there and have to walk and chew gum at the same time, and I don't have them do that. It's one thing at a time. They can then take that and then practice that one skill. I also liken it or compare it to regular conversation. When they are speaking at a meeting, if they are sitting down, they have no problem with that. They can practice these same skills there. Then we graduate to a standing position. We do it in stages.

Now, in my chapter on overcoming nervousness, I talk about a lot of different techniques. One of them is your breathing because when you get nervous, all systems are going. What happens is your adrenaline starts to rush and you start to speed up and you don't know what you are doing, so breathe deeply and slowly because that will slow down and calm down your system and get you ready. Another technique is to go there early. Go on site an hour early. Get to know the people so that you're not facing a sea of strangers, but you feel like you have a few people on your side. You have a bit of a relationship there. Start the presentation with a question if you're that nervous. Because immediately what that does is it takes the focus off of you. A lot of people are uncomfortable in the spotlight. They tell me, "Oh, all eyes are on me." Well, then take the eyes off of you and put it on them. You do that by asking questions and getting a little bit of dialogue going.

Another technique that works is to rehearse your presentation in the actual room. I can't tell you scientifically why that works. I do know that when I've arrived early and done the whole presentation in the room before people arrive, my presentations are better. So get a feel for the room, take charge, rehearse, rehearse, rehearse. There is no substitute for preparation. In fact I tell people that its 90 percent preparation and 10 percent delivery. That is a good formula to keep in mind. Get a good night's sleep and don't over rehearse. Let it go. Give yourself positive programming. By that I mean, actually take time visualizing the outcome that you want. See yourself in a positive light. Keep the audience clapping. Hear the confidence in your voice. See the evaluations that are written in positive terms. See people smiling and nodding their heads and then say a few positive things to yourself such as I am confidant. I can do this. Because people sabotage their success not only in speaking and communicating, but just in life in general by saying negative things to themselves and holding negative thoughts. This is the key.

Wright

In your book you dedicate a full chapter to listening. Tell us what listening has to do with giving a spoken presentation.

DiResta

Listening has everything to do with giving a spoken presentation. I think the mistake that many communicators make is they think that it's a one-way process. I'm going to get up there and I'm going to WOW the crowd. When you come from that mindset, you are self-centered. You're not going to be the most effective impactful speaker that you can be until you turn your focus on others. Part of the listening is in your preparation work: asking the questions, hearing what this audience really needs from you whether it is one person or a thousand, and then developing your presentation or your talk according to what I call listener-centered communication which is starting with what's important to the listener not with your agenda. This is the big mistake in meetings. People talk about what they want instead of finding a way to grab attention by focusing on their needs, their issues, their hot buttons, and their goals. Then listening is also on a non-verbal level. When you have good eye contact, which is one of the visual confidence skills of speaking and communicating, you are watching for those non-verbal messages, and that helps you to pace your audience. When you are looking and you are listening, when you are hearing a lot of coughing and rustling, it means they are restless. They are not 100 percent with you, so change your pace. Maybe you need to pick up the speed a bit. Maybe you need to slow it down. Maybe you need to take a break and ask a question. That's where the listening comes in.

Wright

When you consider the makeup of audiences in today's world, are they any different from audiences of the say 80s and 90s?

DiResta

I think there is a bit of a difference. One of the differences is the times in which we live. People are on information over load. I often ask people, "How many of you can bear to read one more e-mail this morning?" It's harder to capture their attention. You are competing with so many more messages. Think about tele-marketers and all the spam you get, so it's really a challenge to get up there and capture their attention and keep them with you. Your pace has to be quicker than before. I also teach people media training for those who have to speak to the press or TV. The average sound byte has been reduced from 10 seconds to seven seconds. People, even in their hourly or daily presentations need to speak more in sound bytes. Capture the audience quickly and concisely. That's key. The other thing that's true today more than ever is that we live in a multi-cultural society. Our audiences are from all walks of life and you really do need to be savvy in cross-cultural communications today. So the implications for that are watching the idioms that you use. Minimize the buzzwords. In fact, in my newsletter this month I have an article on abusing buzzwords because it minimizes what the message is. There is something that's going on in some companies. They call it BS Bingo. What happens is, you know when people are at meetings they get bored and play games. BS Bingo works like this: you listen to what management is saying and every time they use one of those buzz words, like *going forward* or *paradigm shift*, you start to write them down in a sequence. When you get enough of them in a row, someone might even shout out "Bingo!" Watch your buzzwords. Watch your idioms. Be very careful about humor, especially with male/female audiences and with different cultures. It's so easy to offend somebody today.

Wright

It sure is. Could you give our readers some tips on how to build a presentation that will keep the attention of their audiences?

DiResta

Yes. A lot of it is doing your homework, really knowing whom your audience is and how they like to listen. I coach people on behavioral communication. That is, first know your own self. Socrates said the unexamined life is not worth living. Know your own style. I know what my style is; I'm what's called a dominant style or high driving style. I like information quick, to the point, and results oriented. When I train people on this and when I give them assessments to find out what their styles are, I then show them how to intuit what other peoples' styles are. Once you know that, you want to select your style in order to be able to communicate the way people can hear and understand. For instance, if you were presenting to senior management, you know it has to be bottom line, to the point. They have very short attention spans. They don't want a lot of details. However, if you are talking to a group of scientists, you had better have a lot of data and details and don't spend a lot of time on long stories and touchy feely material because you will lose credibility with them.

I once was talking to IBM scientists and I was telling them the typical study we all hear about communication, the percentages of visual, vocal, and verbal messages. As soon as I said that someone shot at me, "Whose study is that and when was it done?" You have got to have that information. They want evidence, and they want a lot of truth. It is going to take longer to win over if you don't have that kind of data for them. In communicating it is not just standing on a platform in front of a thousand people. Your platform may be a telephone. Your platform may be the voice mail machine. Your platform may be a meeting. One of the things I say in my book is that we are all public speakers, and we are always on stage. It is knowing how that person needs to receive information. If you don't change the way that you present that information, then you are not going to be successful. So to celebrate your success you need to first know to whom am I speaking and communicating. How do they need to receive information so they can understand it and what do I need to do to change my style? It is very important.

Wright

How important are visual aids when giving a presentation?

DiResta

I think visual aids are very important, but I also think they are over done and over used and we are Power pointed out. Here's why visual aids are important. Most people are visual and if you want people to retain information, studies have shown that when you use a visual, you will increase retention by about 85 percent. By all means use visuals. However, when your whole presentation is PowerPoint and you are just a person reading the slides that will result in low impact. Don't let the visual overtake you. The thing to keep in mind with visual aids is you are the visual and that is the aid. The key word is aid. Use you body, use your voice as a visual. Use demonstrations if it's a smaller group. Take something and make it visual by demonstrating. Let them go through a process. Let them have an "ah ha" experience. Yes, use visuals but don't over do it. Minimize the number of slides that you use.

Wright

Diane, with our *Conversations on Success* book we are trying to encourage our readers to be better, to live better and be more fulfilled by listening to the examples of our guests. Is there anything or anyone in your life that has made a difference for you and helped you to become a better person?

DiResta

Yes, I'd say both parents were very strong advocates of education, higher education, and I have no regrets regarding any amount of time or money I've spent on any kind of education and self-development. I really think that education equals enlightenment and the more we can educate people, the more successful they are going to be and the better our society will be. There was also a woman whose name was Rose Erickson, and she was a psychic. I had gone for a reading one time and she said one thing that changed my life. What she said to me was, "Life is a school. Learn from it." When she said this, things were not going well and I was not feeling successful. From that point on I always looked for the lesson. That has really helped me not only to grow but also to go through difficult times because it's not focusing on why me but what is the lesson here. What can I learn? It really is in keeping with what I have been taught and the value I have about education and learning. I think that is so important for people to continually look for that lesson and learn and get themselves to higher levels. The other major mentor has been the National Speakers Association. It really helped me change the way I think. It has put me in front of so many different motivators and educators and business people. It has been a great on going education for me.

Wright

What do you think makes up a great mentor? In other words, are there characteristics that mentors seem to have in common?

DiResta

I think mentors love developing people. They get juiced by that, and it is not about ego, it is about the other person. When you can be a resource or help somebody and you can watch them grow and you see the efforts of your work, what could be more rewarding than that? So I think first and foremost, they are people who really love developing and helping people grow. They usually are people who have a certain expertise in a particular area and are willing to share it. They are people who are not going to do it for you but will coach you along. They are people who will challenge you. I think mentors also challenge you. They build your confidence. They believe in you. To me the greatest mentors are people who really believe in your own abilities.

Wright

It could be in the last chapter in your book. I don't remember, but I think it was the last chapter. You write about special speaking situations. One of the things that really impressed me that you kept saying through the entire book was that everyone is a public speaker. In this chapter I remember you even covered things like leaving voice mail messages. I run a business now where I have about 10 people on the telephone almost all day long. In today's culture when you make 100 calls you really only reach about 30 percent of the people. So it is really important to send a message that will get the interest of the person or you will never get a return call.

DiResta

Right.

Wright

So these things like leaving voice messages and even doing team presentations. You talked about doing team presentations at work and sharing meetings and things like that. Could you give us some examples of things that might come up even if our readers and listening audience is not a "professional speaker," could you give us a little bit about what you were talking about in that chapter?

DiResta

In special situations?

Wright

Yes.

DiResta

Again your success depends on how well you can present yourself and your message, and how valuable you are. In that regard we are all public speakers. The big myth about public speaking is that "I'm not a public speaker because I don't give a written speech on a stage in front of 100 people." My goal is to redefine public speaking. Any time you are speaking outside of your home, that's the public. Or even if you are in your home and you are leaving a voice mail that is your public. Any time you are going beyond family and friends you are speaking to the public. How well you do that will determine how successful you are. When you are leaving a voice mail you can actually communicate to people that they should not call you back. The way you do that is by leaving long, winding messages where people delete or fast forward. I have worked with people at a director level because they were leaving messages that were so long—a minute and a half—and their boss couldn't stand it. Or you are not leaving your phone number. A good idea is to give your phone number at the beginning of your message and at the end for two reasons. One, some people don't want to hear the whole message they just want the number so they can call you back. And sometimes they don't have a pen handy so if you wait until the end and give it again you are assured that they get it.

There are a lot of things that people do that sabotage their success using voice mail. People will judge you by the way that you leave a message. If you don't sound confident, or if you don't sound prepared and you are saying a lot of "ums" and "ahs," people will choose not to return your call. If you don't pronounce peoples' names correctly, they'll think that you didn't do enough homework. Those are some of the things that get in the way of the message. I know when I was looking for an office assistant at one point I would screen them on the phone. If they weren't articulate and clear, I wouldn't call them for an interview *because they were representing me.* Now one of the things that is important in business is we don't spend enough or we don't pay receptionists enough. I don't think we train them well enough. One company that, I think, has the right idea took her receptionist and gave her a new title. She called her V.P. of First Impressions. She's right. That is your front line and your company is that receptionist. You judge that company by the person who answers the phone. So we need to train people better and we need to pay them better because they really are V.P.'s of First Impressions.

Wright

I know exactly what you are talking about. It's all you can do in written form too. I get these letters now with mail merging. I get letters that look like they are personal letters but they will say "Good Morning, Mr. David E. Wright." And I am thinking I am on someone's mailing list. If you could have a platform and tell our readers something that you feel would help or encourage them, what would you say to them?

DiResta

Something that would help and encourage them?

Wright

Yes.

DiResta

Well, I think that, I shouldn't say think. I know we all have the power to be our best, and power is not something outside of us. It lives within us. We need to learn how to tap into it. Once you tap into that power you are able to project what's already there. You are going to be much more successful. One, believe in yourself; believe that you have that power. Two, get a coach or a mentor who can help bring out your best and never stop learning. The key to success is learning and education.

Wright

What a great conversation. I really did learn a lot myself today.

DiResta

Thank you.

Wright

Today we have been talking to Diane DiResta. She is the author of *Knockout Presentations, How To Deliver Your Message with Power, Punch And Pizzazz,* and she does a great job not only in her book but in conversation as well. You mentioned your newsletter. Is that something that our readers can get online?

DiResta

Absolutely, it is called Impact Player. It comes out monthly. It is free, all they have to do is go to my website at www.DiResta.com and subscribe on line.

Wright

Go to www.DiResta.com.

DiResta

Right.

Wright

Great. After this conversation, I'm sure a lot of folks will go to your website to read more in your newsletter. Thank you so much, Diane, for being with us today.

DiResta

Thank you, David.

About The Author

Diane DiResta, president of DiResta Communications, Inc. is an International speaker, coach, and author of Knockout Presentations. (Chandler House Press) Her clients gain practical skills to increase their confidence, credibility, and persuasiveness. Diane holds a Masters degree from Columbia University in Speech Pathology and is past president of the NYC chapter of National Speakers Association. Clients include: AT&T, Chase Manhattan Bank, JP Morgan, Merck, NASA, and the NBA. Media exposure includes: CNN, Bloomberg radio, Investors Business Daily, and NY Times.

Diane DiResta

DiResta Communications, Inc.

PO Box 140714

Stanton Island, New York 10314

Phone: 718.273.8627

Fax: 718.447.7720

Email: diane@diresta.com

Website: www.diresta.com

Chapter 4

MARCUS ENGEL

THE INTERVIEW

David E. Wright (Wright)

Today we are talking to Marcus Engel. He is a professional speaker and author who empowers and inspires his audiences to overcome adversity, commit to higher goals and make intelligent choices through the use of his personal, life-changing story. As an 18-year-old college freshman, Marcus was blinded and nearly killed when a drunk driver struck the car in which he was riding. Through 300 hours of reconstructive facial surgery, 2 years of rehab, and thousands of hours of soul searching, Marcus remained committed to his goal of returning to college and reclaiming his life. Please welcome Marcus Engel to *Conversations on Success*.

Marcus Engel (Engel)

Thank you.

Wright

So, you were a typical teenager just after a typical fun-filled night with friends. What happened then?

Engel

At that time, I was an average 18-year-old college freshman just out for an evening with friends. It was my first weekend home from Southwest Missouri State University and I was delighted that a friend had gotten tickets for a St. Louis Blues hockey game. Following the game, our vehicle was struck broadside by a car traveling nearly twice the speed limit. The other driver was highly intoxicated and driving in the wrong lane.

Upon impact, all four of us were thrown from the car. I have no recollection of those moments of impact and flying through the air, but I soon returned to consciousness and found myself lying face down in the pavement and feeling my facial bones crushed.

Wright

Goodness. When you reached the hospital did you have any idea how badly you had been injured?

Engel

I did not. I knew I was hurt, but I wasn't aware just how close to death I was. I had broken every bone in my face and those injuries caused severe swelling from the neck up. By the time I reached the emergency room, just a few minutes after the crash, the swelling was so intense that I was starting to suffocate. The trauma physicians were forced to cut an emergency tracheotomy into my throat to create an alternative breathing passage. This meant for the next three weeks I was unable to speak. The next morning, I woke up almost totally void of all five senses and unable to even ask the question, "What happened?"

Wright

So, you were unable to see, you can barely hear, taste, or smell and your body is still the same, so how did you communicate if you were unable to talk?

Engel

Improvisation. I reverted back to childhood and remembered watching Kermit the Frog on Sesame Street. Kermit used his magic pointing finger to draw letters on the TV screen in an effort to teach kids to read. I tried to trace letters and words onto my hospital sheets, but that was impossible for my doctors and nurses to read. My aunt, a nurse who immediately came to town as soon as she heard the news of my crash, gave me a tablet and paper in order to write out my communications. For the next three weeks, my only means of conversation came through a pencil and paper, all the conversations about my medical condition, the heartfelt affirmations with my family and friends, everything. Those handwritten notes encompass that horrible experience better than any words I could write and are so powerful that they have been transcribed into my book to give the reader a visual image of the severity of the situation.

Wright

By the way, did anybody in the car have on a seatbelt?

Engel

With 110 percent certainty I cannot say for sure. I was raised to always wear my seat belt and it was a habit I was accustomed to. However, I don't believe that specific night I was wearing the belt. For whatever reason; a different car, the cold, the fact we had a bit of car trouble, I'm fairly sure I simply forgot to put it on. Since we were all thrown from the car and I was void of any bruising across my chest and stomach which would indicate restraint, it is a logical assumption to say I did not have my safety belt on, but I just don't remember for sure.

Wright

When the doctors first told you that you would be permanently blind, what did you think?

Engel

Being informed that you will never see again is a pretty hard thing for an 18-year-old kid to swallow. At first, I didn't want to believe it and kept asking the doctors if there were any eye exercises I could do to regain my sight, but I was told that no operations, medications, or treatments could bring back my vision. Throw in the fact I was in constant and horrific pain from all the broken facial bones and the situation deteriorates even further. Strangely enough, that pain was actually a bit of a blessing. Blindness actually took a back seat to how badly I was hurting. I couldn't really worry about the fact I couldn't see when I was facing a 25-hour facial reconstruction the next day.

Wright

So you were 18, facing hundreds of hours of surgery, you're blind, your future's totally up in the air, most people would want to give up, don't you think?

Engel

Sure, and I also wanted to give up for a while. Having one's life altered completely is one thing, but the knowledge of just how much physical pain will have to be endured is something just as difficult. At first, I wasn't sure it was worth the battle.

Wright

So what made you decide to move on?

Engel

First, my friends and family. If I gave up, it would hurt them more than me. They hadn't given up on me and I could not give up on them. Plus, I had to face the facts; I had a lot of life left to live. The idea of sitting around for the rest of my life feeling sorry for myself wasn't very appealing, nor was the idea of having someone wait on me constantly. I wanted my old life back, or at least as close to it as I could ever have again. Lying in that hospital bed, I committed myself to try to recapture what I had before; the life of an average college student.

Plus, one of the major influences that got me through those times came from a pretty unlikely source. Since I could do nothing for myself, I would just lay in bed, thinking about my life and listening to music. One night, I got a little inspiration from Bob Dylan. I was listening to a compilation of songs when I heard Dylan sing the lyric, 'negativity don't pull you through'. I remember thinking that his words were such a great piece of advice and feeling as though they had been written for me. After all, I couldn't operate on myself, I couldn't do the physical and occupational therapy for myself, but I knew I still controlled one thing that no one else could touch: my attitude. Upon hearing Dylan's advice, I began to focus on the positive aspects I still had: my friends, family and the ability to choose how I viewed my circumstances.

Wright

You had some amazing people around you who were there for you every step of the way, but what about the medical personnel? They played a big part in your life during this time, didn't they?

Engel

Absolutely! Doctors, nurses, and therapists were the icing on the cake above the support I had from friends and family. Nurses and physicians really helped me by not treating me as just another patient they had to care for as part of their job. Some even treated me like a member of their own family. I think the reason for this incredible care was because they would come into my room and see this battered, beaten 18-year-old kid who could have just as easily been their son, brother, cousin or friend. I was never treated as just some anonymous patient who would soon be out of the hospital and on his way to a full recovery; quite the opposite. In fact, a decade later, I am still in contact with several members of my rehab team. I will never be able to thank them enough for the interest they took in helping me get back on my feet.

Wright

Once you were released from the hospital, your book describes a year of homebound recovery, and a year is a long time for anybody no matter what the age. It must have been especially difficult for you to handle all that time because of your being such a young person. What sorts of things did you fill your time with and how did these factors help motivate you?

Engel

During much of that year, it was necessary for me to be attached to a feeding tube. Without the ability to walk or eat solid food, I was forced to find new and different ways to escape from my reality. The main way I did this was through reading. I would devour a new book practically every day and I always tried to take a bit of inspiration from every piece of literature; no matter the genre of the work, I seemed to find something useful from the words of the authors.

Wright

Let me interrupt you a minute.

Engel

Sure.

Wright

You said you were reading. I thought you were blind.

Engel

You are correct. I was and am blind, but reading was just another adaptation for me. I would get all of my books on tape from the Library of Congress and listen to everything from the classics to novels to religious writings.

Wright

I thought that was the way it was. I've been listening to books on tape for years and years.

Engel

Sure, it was one of the more minor adaptations I had to make. After a while, reading books on tape became just as natural as the way I'd read before I lost my sight. When I wasn't reading during that year of recovery, I was taking lessons in adaptive daily living techniques from a vocational rehab teacher who was also blind. She gave me a lot of inspiration because I had never met a blind person before I met Judy. When she taught me these adaptive skills, I just thought it was absolutely amazing how well she could do practically everything I'd done when I was sighted. That really made me think, "Well, if she can do it, I can do it, too!" More importantly, she was not someone who felt sorry for herself. She just lived her life being happy with who she was. Blind or sighted, she showed me that no matter the circumstances, you don't have to feel sorry for yourself nor be down about what has happened in the past.

Wright

After that year was completed, what came next? What was the next step along your journey?

Engel

The next step was a move to Denver, Colorado to begin an adult rehabilitation school. This was a program designed to challenge blind adults and teach them adaptive daily living skills on a consistent basis; Nine hours a day, every day of the week. Each minute was filled with learning Braille, computer skills, adaptive cooking techniques and, even in the evenings and on the weekends, living alone in an apartment off-campus gave a great exposure to how I'd be living once I returned to college. The program at the Colorado Center for the Blind was supposed to last 18 months, but I graduated from the program after only five months.

Wright

So you graduate from rehab school after five months when the program generally lasts 18. What made you so determined to push yourself through the program?

Engel

Ever since laying in that hospital bed, my goal had always been to get myself back to college as quickly as possible. I stayed focused on that goal, worked incessantly to accomplish it and really became a workaholic, so to speak, at acquiring all the adaptive skills and educational techniques I could. The end of the school day did not signal a time off when I could just sit back and put my feet up. Every night, I worked on additional skills, always putting in the overtime hours that would ultimately bring me one step closer to accomplishing my goal. I was pretty amazed myself when, after less than a third of the recommended time at the center, I realized I'd accomplished everything I'd set out to do!

Wright

Now we come to one of the most heart-warming parts of your recovery, the acquisition of your first Seeing Eye Dog, Dasher. Tell us about receiving Dasher and the training, and by the way, who named him Dasher?

Engel

Well, it wasn't me! I chose to receive my guide dog from The Seeing Eye, Inc. located in Morristown, New Jersey. At the beginning of each year, the first litter of puppies all receive names that begin with the letter, "A." The pups from the second litter all receive names that begin with, "B" and so on through the alphabet. Dasher just happened to come from the "D" litter. When I first arrived at Morristown, I thought I would be receiving a dog that would increase my independence and a friend that would allow me to maneuver more easily through crowds on campus.

I didn't realize that he was going to be one of the biggest elements of my emotional recovery, too. For the four weeks of training, we went through every type of traffic situation imaginable; everything from quiet neighborhood streets to the congested thoroughfares of New York City. Dasher also did an incredible job when we trained inside department stores, restaurants, on the subways and trains, everything. He truly loved his "work" and thrived on being on the streets whenever he could. Dasher was with me for over seven years until he went into retirement in the summer of 2002. A month later, I received Carson, also a black lab, who has stepped into the role of my guide and does an excellent job!

Wright

You had a simply amazing coincidence while you were training with Dasher in New Jersey. What was that and how did it affect your life?

Engel

The first night I spent in New Jersey, I met a student from Texas, Ron Graham, who was also receiving his first Seeing Eye dog. I over-heard Ron tell another student that he had lost his sight in a car accident. This immediately intrigued me because in the 18 months that had elapsed since losing my sight, I'd only met one other person who was blinded in a crash. I asked Ron about the loss of his sight and when his wreck had occurred. I nearly fainted when Ron shared the date of his crash, October 9th, the same night as I lost my sight. As I was lying in an intersection in St. Louis, Missouri, Ron was laying in a cotton field outside of Lubbock, Texas, both of us blind and clinging to life.

Wright

My goodness.

Engel

Over 800 miles away from each other, we were experiencing nearly identical circumstances. The more I thought about it, the more amazing it became. #1, it is pretty unique to be traumatically blinded in a car crash. #2 we both decided to acquire a dog from the same school. And# 3, that we showed up for the same month long training session. There were a huge number of "coincidences" surrounding our meeting that all seemed to point in the same direction. It was meant for Ron and I to meet. I consider our introduction to be a gift from God—a gift for both of us. At a time in my life when I really needed support and understanding, I was given a new friend who could not only relate to my circumstances, but someone who had experienced almost identical trauma.

Wright

When you left the Seeing Eye, Inc. with your new dog, what happened next?

Engel

My departure from the Seeing Eye, Inc. marked the final leg of the two-year journey back to re-claiming my life and returning to college. I spent a month getting acclimated to Dasher and learning all his movements and quirks as a dog and a guide. Just four weeks after leaving NJ, I moved back into the same residence hall at Southwest Missouri State University and tried to pick up the pieces of my life as a college student. That is when the real emotional re-building process began. I was a shy and insecure 20 year old who was still learning to accept all of the life changes that had recently taken place. Dasher's mere presence gave me social introductions and began friendships that showed me I still had a lot to offer to the world.

Wright

In your book titled *After This...An Inspirational Journey for All the Wrong Reasons*, you described the life changing summer between your freshman and sophomore year of college. Why was that summer so important to reclaiming your life?

Engel

That first year back in college was not an especially happy time for me. While I was learning to live and beginning to adapt to my new life as a blind person, I was still quite self-conscious. There were times I was lonely and other times when I was on top of the world. It was a really emotional year with a lot of ups and downs. At the end of my freshman year, I applied for a staff position at a church camp where I'd spent time attending summer camp as a kid. I wasn't sure I'd be able to pull my weight as a staffer due to my blindness and I hated the thought of having to rely on my co-workers to pick up my slack. I thought there was no way I'd be able to teach kids archery, campfire building, canoeing, and all the usual types of camp events. My fellow staffers believed in me and challenged me to push myself and, after only a week or two, I found myself leading all the activities I never thought I'd be able to do. It was an incredible experience because even when I didn't see the value in myself, the kids that relied on me thought of me as no different than my sighted co-workers. When others viewed me as equal, I had no choice but to also see myself in that way. After all, I couldn't let down the kids that relied on me to be their leader.

Wright

It sounds like camp almost saved your life in a symbolic sense.

Engel

It certainly did. Plus, it educated hundreds and hundreds of kids in a way they could have never learned unless they'd spent time at camp. Every day, Dasher and I would sit down with children and would lead a session, which became known as, "The Marcus and Dasher Show." I would spend an hour talking with the kids about how I had lost my sight and then give them the opportunity to pepper me with any sorts of questions they had about blindness, how Dasher worked, how I lived my life, etc. It was so interesting to see the kids' attitudes change from, "Oh, you're blind. You can't do the things I can," to seeing that there is basically no difference between themselves and me, I just had to do things a little differently.

Wright

You actually, during the time that you were at the camp, saved the life of a camper. How does it feel to know that a child may have died were it not for your help?

Engel

I really didn't consider it a big deal and I just hope someone would do the same thing for me if I needed some help. One day during a primary aged session of camp, I was sitting on the edge of the pool with my legs dangling in the water. Just a few feet in front of me I heard a little girl saying, "Help!" and she actually whispered the word. That was the first time I'd ever heard someone whisper, "Help!" It was obvious she was struggling in water over her head, so I just leaned out in the water and picked her up under the arms. After I stood her up on the deck of the pool, she ran off to re-join her friends and I went back to working on my tan! Just then, one of the lifeguards came up, put a hand on my shoulder and said, "Do you realize you just made the first save of the year?" I didn't understand what he was talking about and denied I'd done anything heroic. After all, she was having trouble and I just helped her out. He laughed and said, "Yeah, but I was getting ready to jump in there with a life preserver and pull her out!" While I didn't think of it as anything great, the staff really bolstered my self-esteem by referring to this for the rest of the summer. It was just another confidence builder and an experience that made the summer so special.

Wright

So, you are now happy in accepting of your life. You've readjusted to a world now as a blind person? When did you begin sharing your story and inspiring audiences around the country?

Engel

I guess the beginning of my career was providing campers with "The Marcus and Dasher Show." Those informal small group sessions evolved into a career that truly began when I was asked to give a commencement address for a graduating class of seniors at my alma mater. I was only 22 and really didn't feel I was qualified to have such an honor. After all, I hadn't found a cure for cancer, made a million dollars or really done anything significant with my life other than a return to college. However, after delivering that speech and sharing aspects of my life, there were so many people who congratulated me and said my words had changed their lives. The sheer number of responses made me wonder if I could speak for a living. As soon as I made that decision, all the pieces seemed to click into place and showed me that speaking is what I was meant to do.

Wright

Why did you decide to write your book?

Engel

To help others realize that they can go through the most horrible conditions imaginable and still come out the other side smiling if they can adopt a proper mindset. I hope this book shows them how to focus on the positive and see the good within themselves. I had to learn those things the hard way and I hope others can receive a bit of enlightenment from my experiences. I like to think this book is inspirational for everyone, but can be used as a tool to teach the reader how to implement the elements from my recovery in their own lives. Whether the reader is experiencing something as traumatic as what I went through, or simply having one of the down times we are all prone to, this book can make a difference. I really just want to help people realize their full potential but, if nothing else, the book is an interesting and entertaining story you can get no where else.

Wright

How do you react when your audiences, or your readers for that matter, tell you that your words have changed their lives?

Engel

With humility. It's hard for me to realize how my life and experiences have the power to make changes for others. It is humbling to know that the mission for which I have been chosen has such potential. It's a responsibility I don't take lightly, yet I still marvel that I am so blessed to have been given that opportunity. I just think of myself as living my life, going through the daily motions just like anybody does. When someone tells me that my message has changed their life, I just think, "Wow! Maybe this is the reason that I went through all that horrible suffering. If other people are getting something positive from my message, then it was all worth it."

Wright

You do something very interesting. You know I've been booking speakers and helping speakers make a living now for 13 years and you are kind of set apart because you open yourself up to any and all questions from your audiences and/or your readers. Many people feel that they are prying into your personal life, I would suspect, or maybe even asking you questions that might embarrass or anger you. However, you answer every question with grace and compassion. How do you feel that this benefits your audiences and readers?

Engel

Whether I am giving a presentation or someone is reading my book, my goal is for that person to walk away feeling as though they know me. I don't want them to walk away saying, "I heard a speaker" or "I read this speaker's book," but instead, I want them to have the experience of meeting me and becoming acquainted with me. To make that personal connection or form that friendship will carry my message and lessons for years to come. Whenever I give an audience or a reader the ability to ask me any kind of question, whether it's about blindness, the crash, my Seeing Eye Dog, or how I live my daily life, that gives them a chance to get to know me personally. That's the message that will stick with them a lot longer than just having heard a speech or having read a book. When I lost my sight, I had never met another blind person. I want people all around the world to be a lot more educated about blindness and the ways of the blind than I was at 18. If I can open myself to their questions, that eliminates a tiny bit more of ignorance in the world.

Wright

What motivates you now? What truths do you live by when you get discouraged especially, as anyone in life will? How do you deal with your bad days?

Engel

My bad days are few and far between. I've learned how to positively deal with any adversity that comes my way. I don't allow myself to have a bad day, but I will occasionally allow myself to have a bad morning or an afternoon. Then, at the end of a couple of hours, I pull myself up by the bootstraps and get on with it. What still motivates me is the advice from Bob Dylan, 'negativity don't pull you through.' When I run into an obstacle, I know focusing on that adversity is not going to get me past it and closer to my goal. One other thing that really inspires me is a lesson I learned from my high school principal when I was just 16. One afternoon after football practice, I backed my car into his and experienced my first fender bender. Although I was upset and nervous over hurting his car, he shook my hand and gave me a piece of advice I've never forgotten. "Marcus, there are so many things in this world you can't change. This little fender bender is just one of the things you can. Change the things you can and don't worry about the rest because there's nothing you can do about them anyway." "Change the things you can" is another motto I live by.

Wright

As you were talking about having hours instead of days, I remember the old line about the man who said he was when he got married it was going to be early in the morning so that if it didn't work out he wouldn't blow the whole day.

Engel

(Laughs) I guess there's some truth in every joke!

Wright

Let me ask you a question.

Engel

Sure.

Wright

In the spirit of you allowing me to pry into your life.

Engel

Sure.

Wright

The person who hit you broadside, I know I used to do some work with MADD (Mothers Against Drunk Drivers) and I found that your story, not your life story but at least the accident, is a very typical one. Whatever happened to the man?

Engel

Criminally or physically?

Wright

Both.

Engel

Physically, virtually nothing. I think he sprained his knee, but nothing more. The criminal aspect is tedious. Of the four of us riding in the car, three of us were hurt badly enough to bring charges against the drunk driver. In the state of Missouri that adds up to three counts of second-degree assault, each count could carry a maximum sentence of seven years. Of the potential 21 years he could have received, the flawed aspects of the criminal justice system in our country saw fit to sentence the offender to 120 days in prison.

Wright

That's also a typical story.

Engel

Unfortunately, it is. Sentences have gotten stricter over the last decade, but there are still plenty of cases such as mine that make a mockery of the legal system in our country. When I take questions from my audiences, I often get the questions, "Are you bitter towards the drunk driver?" or "Do you want revenge?" My answer to both is, "No, absolutely not." Getting angry over my experiences or focusing on how the offenders life could mirror mine is a downward spiral I refuse to step into. I use my energies to create an even better life for myself, not for focusing on how his life can be hurt. Really, there is no other way to live!

Wright

Marcus, you have an amazing and unforgettable story. I really appreciate you giving us a glimpse of your incredible life. I'm sure no one will walk away from reading this book and listening to this interview that having learned something that helped them on their life's journey as well. I really do appreciate you taking this time with me today.

Engel

It's my pleasure and once again I will leave my world and my life open up to your readers. If they have any questions or comments, they can feel free to view my website at *www.marcusEngel.com* or drop me an e-mail to *marcus@marcusEngel.com.* I would be more than happy to answer whatever questions your readers may have.

Wright

We have been talking today to Marcus Engel. He is a professional speaker and an author of a great book that you need to buy, who empowers and inspires his audiences to overcome adversity, commit to higher goals, and make intelligent choices through the use of just what he did today, telling his life changing story. Again, Marcus, thank you so much.

Engel

Thank you.

About The Author

At 18, Marcus Engel was blinded and traumatically injured at the hands of a drunk driver. Through hundreds of hours of reconstructive surgery, two years of rehab and training with one Seeing Eye dog, Marcus remained committed to his goal of returning to college and re-claiming his life. Marcus Engel now empowers and inspires audiences to overcome adversity, commit to higher goals and make intelligent choices through the use of his personal, life-changing story.

Marcus Engel

938 N. Taylor

St. Louis, Missouri 63122

Email: marcus@marcusEngel.com

Website: www.marcusEngel.com

Chapter 5

DERRICK KEITH WATKINS, M.S.W

THE INTERVIEW

David E. Wright (Wright)

Today we're talking with Derrick Watkins who, for more than ten years, has been helping people find their true purpose by realizing their potential in order to fulfill their dreams. Derrick's story of rising from a three bedroom apartment in a housing project to becoming a human achievement specialist, face to face communicator, and motivational speaker has inspired thousands of people. This impressive journey of success over poverty, fear of rejection, self-doubt, and family addiction uniquely qualifies him as an expert in the area of human achievement and personal development. His story and the dynamic way he shares it demonstrates the true power of focused will power over obstacles. Derrick motivates audiences to develop their talents and love for life, which will be their ticket out of self-doubt and fear. His memorable personal stories and experiences in human achievement and face to face communication will help your people see how they can transform obstacles into opportunities and failure into triumph. Derrick graduated from New Jersey City University with a Bachelor's degree in communication and received his Master's degree in social work from Rutgers University. He holds certification in Neuro Linguistic Programming, Business Coaching, Handwriting Analysis and Conflict Resolution and has been trained in relationship coaching. In addition, Derrick is a member of the National Speaker's Association and the National Association of Business Coaches. Derrick, welcome to *Conversations on Success*.

Derrick Watkins (Watkins)

Thank you, David. I am glad to be here.

Wright

Why did you become a relationship communications coach and a handwriting expert?

Watkins

Well, there was a time where I was having difficulty truly communicating, not only with people but also with myself. One of the things that I discovered was that communication was not only the key to success; it was the key to lasting successful relationships. I became a Handwriting expert because I needed answers to why my marriage did not work. I have always been able to communicate with people, but for some reason I was having a difficult time communicating with my wife. So, in an attempt to understand personalities and how they differ, I began studying Handwriting Analysis and it has truly changed my life.

Wright

So, you did it as much for yourself as you did it for others?

Watkins

Yes, I did. Communication, in my opinion, is the key to successful and lasting relationships. I became a relationship coach and handwriting expert because not only did I want to be able to communicate better, I also wanted to understand why people communicate the way they do. When I was married, I wish I had known some of the things I know now. I think a lot of people get married just for the event, but they never sit down and talk about how to be a husband or a wife. If more people spent time talking about what type of husband they want and what type of wife they want, maybe when they finally decide to tie the knot, so to speak, they will have a lasting and loving relationship.

Wright

It makes sense. What are the four P's of successful communication that you talk about?

Watkins

The four P's actually represent Proper Communication Prevents Poor Presentation. After becoming certified in Neuro-Linguistic Programming (NLP), I discovered that most people spend a lot of time listening to the words. I'm sure you've heard someone say to you, David, "I love you," and you said to them, "No, you don't." It's not the words that people are listening to, it's how they say it and the body language in which they represent the way they say the words.

What I discovered was that after studying numerous reports on communication, and reading a study by Professor Morabian out of UCLA , 55 percent of the way we communicate is through our body language. We communicate 38 percent of the time using our tone of voice and 7 percent of the time we are communicating using our voice. To have a successful relationship personally or professionally, we have to begin to pay more attention to all three of these areas.

Wright

That's interesting. Do you use a lot of body language communication skills in your workshops?

Watkins

Absolutely. It's interesting because people tend to take for granted their body language, the tonality of their voices and the posture with which they deliver their words. If people spent more time in recognizing how they are standing, looking at how they are speaking when they are one on one with someone-particularly with someone of the opposite sex-they'd be able to get their point across and make sure that they were understood. One of the things that they say in NLP is you are responsible for your level of communication regardless of the information you get back. When you are communicating, it is your responsibility to make sure that the person that you are communicating with understands you. There is that universal sign that people don't understand you, the nodding of the head. When someone nods their head or says, "No, I don't understand," the person who started the conversation has a responsibility to say to the other person, "Let me say this a different way so that you can fully understand what I'm talking about." When I'm doing workshops, particularly with people in business, and we're dealing with supervisors to subordinates, often a subordinate goes to a supervisor and gets information and is assigned a task. The moment that subordinate walks away from the supervisor with that task in mind, if he does not ask any questions, the supervisor automatically assumes that he got it and he knows what to do. Oftentimes people walk away not fully understanding what they're supposed to do. So, when someone who has the skills that I often teach, people pay attention not only to what they say, but also how they say it, and the way they deliver it. It can, most of the time, guarantee that the person they are communicating with actually hears, feels and gets what they are talking about.

Wright

What is rapport and how important is it in relationships?

Watkins

Well, rapport is something that I like to think of particularly when we're dealing with the opposite sex as being connected emotionally, intellectually, and spiritually.

Oftentimes people tend to miss out on how important it is to find people who are just like us. Rapport often is about liking someone who is just like you. Being in rapport is special because you are speaking the same language, even when you don't necessarily understand each other's words. Being in rapport is great because it opens up brand new opportunities, possibilities and relationships that may not have been available before. When you are in rapport with someone, you see things the same way, you laugh at the same things, you tend to discuss and have the same experiences. I like to think that people like people who are like themselves. That's actually the simplest, and most direct definition I can give to rapport. Many people have friends who have been their friends for 10, 15, or 20 years. There are many people who are married 15, 20, 25 years. The reason that they have stayed together for so long or been married for so long is because they're in rapport. Every movement that they make is rhythmic; every movement that they make is balanced. They may not get along all the time but even when they're angry they're still in rapport, and the other person tries to understand fully why they're angry. Achieving ultimate rapport, or finding someone who is just like you, is definitely a key to a lasting relationship.

Wright

Do you believe that opposites attract?

Watkins

I believe that opposites attract and most people you ask would agree. When people get together and they meet one another and they could be in a social club and the person starts to talk and you say, "I really like this guy or girl." But then after six or seven months of liking this guy or girl, you discover that you don't like the fact that he leaves the toilet seat up all the time. You don't like the fact that he doesn't open the car door for you. You don't like the fact that he doesn't like to talk when he's watching the football game or the basketball game. You don't like the fact that she doesn't cook. Or, you don't like the fact that she doesn't clean like you think she can. This is an opposite that you thought you would be able tolerate when you both came together in the beginning. So, that fine woman or man isn't as fine anymore right? So what do you do? Should you leave or try to work it out? Whatever you decide to do, remember, opposites attract, but don't last.

Wright

That makes sense. Why are positive relationships so important?

Watkins

Positive relationships are important because you have to understand that we tend to go into many relationships "just because." Now what do I mean by "just because?" Just because I'm lonely. Just because I don't have any friends. Just because I need a man or woman. I think positive relationships are those that bring quality to your life, not drama. See, I am a person who knows how to live a drama-free life. I try not to develop any relationships that are mixed with people who don't offer me an opportunity to grow. I think people are sick and tired of meeting people who are emotionally draining. When people are frustrated at home, and they do not like their jobs, this is probably a result of the poor relationships that they have in their lives. That not only includes professional that includes personal. Whenever I'm doing training or coaching or mentoring, regardless if its relationship coaching or even handwriting analysis, I often tell people to make sure that the relationships that you have in your life are positive. If the people in your life are bringing drama into your life, you have to make a decision if you want to keep those people in your life.

Wright

So the decision would be to walk away or help them change?

Watkins

The decision would be to try and understand why people are the way they are and that you can't possibly change them. I think we spend a lot of time trying to make our negative relationships into positive ones because of the fear of being lonely. It's okay to be alone, but you choose to be lonely. Everyone is alone at one point in their life, but lonely is another thing. What we need is to spend a lot of time and effort managing our personal emotions as well as managing the people that we associate with. I'm a firm believer that there will be people who will come into your life to offer you something or rob you of something. The one thing that has to be understood is we are responsible for the people we attract.

What I often here is "I can't find someone I can trust anymore." Trust, I believe, is test plus time equaling trust. What this means is over a certain amount of time, there will be a number of different tests that people will pass in order for you to totally trust them. There are a lot of people out there who have given up on the ability to trust because they've been hurt so often in the past. Because of this, many people are scared to open up their lives to people they have just met instantly. When you have so many different setbacks and setups in your life, you tend not to be open to many new and interesting relationships. So right now, people are cautious about trying new things, finding and starting new relationships and going to different places that are new because they are fearful of being hurt again. That's what stops people from finding positive relationships. I believe that positive relationships are out there and in order for you to find one and grow, you have to understand that you have to take some risks. With risk comes setbacks, but with every setback there will be a reward for your efforts on the other side. My mother always told me, "Derrick just remember that with every burden there's a blessing. Just keep moving. Keep going and keep growing."

Wright

Derrick, who are the people who helped you get where you are today?

Watkins

The people who helped me get where I am today are mostly family. I have a very large family including friends who have stuck by me when things were great and when things were bad. My five brothers and I were born and raised in one of the toughest housing projects in Jersey City, New Jersey. My mother and father taught us to be loyal, dependable and responsible. My father was tough. As the disciplinarian, he taught me and my brothers how to be men. My mother taught us how to be sympathetic to women and be understanding to women, their needs and to understand that women are different from men. I believe that men are definitely from Mars and women are from Venus. Because of our differences we have to learn to respect women and their abilities to provide a safe and secure home for themselves and others. And woman have to respect a mans need to be needed even though a woman has expressed that she does not need a man to take care of her. There is one other person who was a major influence on my life who died a few years ago by the name of Stanley Wanagail. Stanley was very intelligent, very authentic, and very genuine. He did wonders with juvenile delinquents. Stanley had a way of talking to you that would make you think and invest time into asking, "Hmm, did he really say that? Did he really mean that or was he trying to say something else?" Stanley was a great artist, a great man, and one of the only guys I knew who would walk around in the dead of winter with no socks on.

Wright

Strange.

Watkins

But he was brilliant. He spent a lot of time investing in self. He didn't have a lot of clothes; he only had one pair of jeans. He didn't have a lot of friends. Whenever he was hungry, he would reach into his back pocket for a piece of bread and that was all he ate. He called this food in his pocket, "the food of champions." He was a very strange man, but it was his uniqueness that attracted me to him because he was not only a smart man, but he was living his life the way he wanted to live it. Up until the day he died in his house, by himself, on his couch, in his sleep, he lived his life to the fullest. I miss him.

Wright

It sounds like you miss him. We talk about achievement, success, and all of those things that mean we have made it. What do you think it takes to make it?

Watkins

There are three things it takes to make it in life. First of all it takes positive relationships. You've got to keep people in your life that will influence you in a way that you'll grow. The second thing it takes is focus and most importantly, you must have a plan. We spend too much time going through life casually. Those individuals who are casual about life one day become a casualty. When I am coaching people, I often ask, "Where do you expect to be five years from now, ten years from now, twenty years from now? What type of family do you expect to have? Do you want a family? Where do you expect to be in your work?" The answer to these questions is always vague and unclear.

The thing to remember most about the last question is your work and your job are two different things. Most people don't know this. They get work mixed up with job. I tend to think that a job is something that you do just to pay the bills, put food on your table and clothes on your back. But work is the thing that God has given you to do that is special. The thing that separates you from the pack. Your work is the thing that you love to do. The thing that you would do for free and people will pay you to do because you are not just good but great. People will pay you. And your responsibility is to just say thank you.

A job is something that you do just to get by. So, it is important to keep making plans as to what you would like to do with your life, how much time it will take you to get it done and who you must keep around you in order to make your dreams a reality. Another thing you must have is a vision. Dream a little bit. We stop dreaming as we get older. I love talking to my daughter, Da'jah, who often tells me how she wants to be a doctor, a lawyer, a nurse; I mean she bounces back and forth from one thing to the other. But I remind her everyday to dream, to keep dreaming and never give up regardless of how old we are; we should always allow ourselves to visualize what we want to be. I think we've given up on that part of our lives just because the daily routine of life itself has taken a toll on us. The thing that people forget is that life is hard, it is not easy. Because it's hard, every opportunity to make an accomplishment and get something done makes it worthwhile. So, yes, life is hard. You succeed at something, you fail at something. But every experience is an opportunity to learn.

Everyone has that one moment in life where something happens in which you will never forget that experience. We say, "Wow, I remember when I _____." I call this experience a "defining moment." What is a defining moment? A defining moment is that thing that no matter how old you get you will always remember. It is something that is special to you, that is dear to you, and that you will never ever forget. I can always remember at least a couple of defining moments in my life that have helped make me the person that I am today. I revisit those moments every now and then when I feel that I can't make it, when I can't get on or can't get some of the things done that I need to- particularly when coaching and training other people, mentoring people, writing books, writing articles and doing speeches. Every now and then when I don't feel like doing it, I just remember that last defining moment when I did something so well that the people I was working with said, "Derrick, can you come back and do that for us again? I really appreciate the work that you've done for me."

Wright

In your workshops you talk about living life with purpose and refer to the two keys of life. Could you share those with us?

Watkins

Sure. I believe that the first key to a successful and fulfilling life is growth. Personal growth is the most important key to my life. As we go through life, we are either growing or slowly dying. When I am speaking and training, it often amazes me when I ask if someone in the audience reads self-help books and 60-70 percent of the people don't raise their hands. People often claim they want to be wealthy and they don't want to be lonely, but they never attend a seminar on how to get rich or how to find the perfect mate. I truly believe that in order for anyone to make a life that is spiritually, emotionally and intellectually balanced, you must read more, do more and be around people who will challenge you to grow. Do something that's going to make you grow. People tend to take jobs or go into relationships, in particular, where they don't grow. When you're talking about being married to either your work or to a mate, you sometimes fall into a comfort zone. What's a comfort zone? A comfort zone is a level of comfort where you are okay with things just moving the way they're moving. But in order for you to grow, you have to always find something that will challenge you and your relationship. I think what happens is that people get threatened by growth. In relationships, there is always one person that outgrows the other person. This is one of the toughest things to accept in relationships. Two people will not come into a relationship and be at the same plateau at the same time. One person will rise, the other person will rise behind them, then that person will rise and the other person will rise behind them. What happens a lot is that people become threatened by the other person's growth. They don't understand that growth is what you want because that is what defines your life.

When people die and they walk into the funeral and the pastor says, "Is there anyone here who can say something good about this person who has moved on?" You want people to say some things about you that are truthful, not things that have been created because you got stuck. You want people to say something that you've actually done. There are too many people that are buried in what I believe is the richest place in the world, the cemetery, who haven't written that book that they thought about, haven't published that article that they thought about, haven't made that movie that they talked about for years because they got stagnated. They became afraid to grow. And the thing that stops people from growing is the fear of the unknown. That thing that says, "Once I do this, what's going to happen to me?" But that's the thing, Dave that should get them excited. The fact that I don't know is the thing that motivates me to keep moving forward. The fact that what's on the other side of this fence may not necessarily be grass, it could be astro turf, but I have the ability to turn that astro turf into grass.

The second key to life is contribution. I am always willing to give my time, effort and my money to people, places and things that are in need. This is the most important success secret that people overlook. There are many people that have dedicated their entire lives to helping those that are in need. Mahatma Gandhi, Mother Teresa and Martin Luther King, just to name a few, have made a major contribution to society, as we now know it. Your ability to be willing to put aside your dreams in order to help someone else will repay double if you take the risk. I often hear that a successful relationship requires that each person to contribute 50 percent in order for the relationship to be successful. Well, if I am only giving 50 percent, whom do I give the other 50 percent to? Relationships require each person contributing 100 percent of their efforts 100 percent of the time.

Wright

If I could use the analogy of life being like a sporting event, football, basketball, or hockey, what do you think keeps people on the bench?

Watkins

People stay on the bench because they don't want to play a role in the team concept. When people come together in a relationship, whether it is business or family, there are certain roles that each person has to be willing to play. I remember back in the day I was a Chicago Bulls fan. I loved Michael Jordan. To this day I still love him. What helped the Chicago Bulls win six championships was the way that each person accepted their role. There were no great shooters on this team. They were absolutely not the best team on paper. They had probably the best two players. But what Phil Jackson did was he gave them a system that they believed in. What has to happen in business, relationships and families is that people have to develop a system that everyone believes in. The thing that we must always remember is that there are rules in place to keep order in society, business and families. In the game of life, rules are designed to keep order, structure, and even fairness in place. As a society, we must have rules about traffic, sports and the law. If we don't have these rules, we would be living in total chaos. If the rule in the family is you're going to come together to eat at 6 o'clock p.m. for dinner, everyone has to hold true to the system and the rule. The people who stay on the bench are the ones who are defiant to the system, refuse to live by the rules and lack the ability to understand that this is not about me, this is about us.

In business, when you have a "me attitude" it distracts all of the other people from joining in as one because they say to themselves, "If he can do it and she can do it, I can do it." It only takes one person to ruin it. It doesn't take a lot of people to get off the bench. But it does take a special person to say, "I am willing to do whatever it takes for us to win." One bad apple in the bunch is a bad apple that could possibly put a bad taste in the mouths of everyone and no one will want to taste the fruit of happiness and success again.

Wright

We talked a few minutes ago about the importance of positive relationships. Is it equally important or is it very difficult to maintain positive relationships?

Watkins

It is difficult to maintain positive relationships, I would definitely say, but it's not impossible. Once again, I believe that life is hard and if we understand that and expect certain things not to go our way, we would be able to maintain our relationships. The relationships that are difficult to maintain, particularly when we talk about family—and I like to use the family in terms of personal and professional—are the ones that are self-destructive and emotionally draining.

I recall being in a position of leadership where I taught my staff to not only be positive but to maintain a relationship with each other that is always positive. I often emphasis that you don't have to like each other, but you have to be able to get the job done so that we can go in a direction that says we're doing great work. I often tell people that if you're in leadership and you have your staff developing where they're doing things the way they should be done, and they feel good about what they are doing, this makes others wonder if you as the leader are working at all! It's not that the leader doesn't do much work, it's that the leader has taught his staff so well to respect each other's abilities and jobs that it looks like he's not doing anything. But he's actually doing what he's supposed to: mentoring, coaching, and giving up so much information on how to be just like him, that his staff loves working for him.

I recall having what many people consider an open door policy with my staff regarding any issue, personal or professional. What this did was it gave them the opportunity to see me, not just as their leader, but as someone they can trust personally and professionally. Not like a friend—because you don't want to get too close when you're in leadership. When your staff sees you as a friend, this could make them believe they can get anything from you at anytime. What you want is for them to look at you in a way that says, "If I've got a problem I know I can go talk to Mr. Watkins about it because I know that he will give me a direct and fair assessment of what I should do."

Wright

Why is it important to have a mentor or coach?

Watkins

Since the age of 10, I always played sports. I always had a mentor or coach behind me. My mother was my biggest coach. I can recall one time when I came home from a football game—I only played football one day—I played one Pee Wee Football game and I had had a great game. I walked up to the door and knocked and my mother said, "Hi." I said, "Hello, Ma." She said, "How was the game?" and I said, "The game was great." I wanted to come in the house but she was standing in the doorway and wouldn't move. I said, "What's the matter?" She said, "You can't come in here with those clothes on." I said, "What, the uniform?" She said, "Yeah, you have to take those clothes off. You're not going to track that mud in my house." I said, "But I'm in the hall." We lived in the projects on the second floor and there were people walking up and down the hall. I said, "Ma, I don't have anything on under this." She said, "So?" So I took off my shoulder pads and helmet and dropped them in the hall. All I had on was a tank top tee shirt and my football pants. I said, "How's this?" She said, "No, take it all off." I said, "But ma, all I have on underneath my pants is a jock strap." So, I took off all of my clothes and walk in the house with nothing but a jock strap on and that was the last day I played football. I went back to my coach the next day and I said, "Look, if I've got to go home and strip my uniform in the hall everyday, then this sport is not for me." So, I didn't play football anymore, but I went on to play basketball in high school and college and some semi-pro basketball.

I've always had a coach around me to direct me on how to do things the right way. Not my way, but the right way. What I believe is that a coach or a mentor has experience in the things that you are going through and tends to not necessarily tell you what to do but to give you options. That's what a good coach does. He doesn't tell you what to do; he gives you a different perspective, a different way of looking at things, and options. He says to you, "Based upon all of these things that we've talked about choose the one that best fits you because in the end you have to live with it." That's why it's important to have a coach or mentor.

Wright

There is a famous prayer that talks about accepting the things that you cannot change. How important do you think it is to accept the things you cannot change?

Watkins

In life, we will come across a tremendous amount of challenges and things that we cannot change. In order for you to accept the things you cannot change, you have to realize that you're not supposed to change everything. Everything will not be your way because life isn't fair. Because life isn't fair, every now and then you will have burden that will come across your path, you will have an obstacle that you won't be able to overcome, but if you step back and be still-just relax-and allow yourself to wonder about the best way to deal with this problem, you will recognize that what you're being faced with is just a challenge, it's not the end of the world. Most people have a hard time accepting the things that they cannot change. They fight change. They fight the possibility that something new might work for them. I often ask not why, but why not? Some things are supposed to be that way, not just to test you but also to challenge you to take a different approach. It's like a person hits a wall one, two, maybe three times and realizes that this wall isn't going anywhere because maybe that's where it's supposed to be. Maybe instead of going through the wall you have to walk down the side of the wall to find the easiest way around. Sometimes going through it isn't the way. Sometimes you have to take another direction. I've learned that in my life.

When I got divorced and I really wanted my marriage to work, I realized that it wasn't going to work. It takes two people for a marriage to work. It took me a long time to accept that I was no longer in this relationship that I wanted to have for the rest of my life. Once I realized that I couldn't change what was going on, it was very easy for me to focus on the things that matter the most, which was not only my life but also the life of my daughter. Once I focused on that it was very easy for me to go on. I think most people spend a lot of time in relationships that are bad because they want them to work. They need to realize that it's not that the relationship is bad; it's just that it's not the one for you right now.

Wright

Well, what a great conversation. I've learned a lot today and I have a lot of things to think about. Today we have been talking with Derrick Watkins. For more than ten years he has been helping people find their true purpose by realizing their potential in order to fulfill their dreams. As we have found out today he is really good at it. Thank you so much, Derrick, for being with us on *Conversations on Success*.

Watkins

Thank you, David.

About The Author

Derrick Keith Watkins, M.S.W. is the second oldest of six children reared in one of Jersey City, New Jersey's toughest Housing projects. By combining hard work, persistence and determination, Derrick received his bachelor's degree in Communications from New Jersey City University and his Master's degree from Rutgers University. As a certified NLP Practitioner, Relationship Coach and Handwriting Expert, Derrick is uniquely qualified to motivate audiences to develop their talents and love for life.

Derrick Watkins, M.S.W.
Speak with Power and Passion
918 West Chestnut Street
Union, New Jersey 07083
Phone: 886.206.9066 Ext. 8939
Website: www.derrickkeithwatkins.com

Chapter 6

SANDRA CONTRERAS

THE INTERVIEW

David E. Wright (Wright)

Today we are talking to Sandra Contreras. She has worked in a variety of industries including: construction, manufacturing, health care, accounting and real estate. Her wide range of professional experiences allows her to connect successfully with people from all walks of life and to present her seminars and workshops in a comfortable engaging manner. Sandra has lived in Costa Rica and taken extended visits to Nicaragua and Honduras. She has served as an ambassador on two People-To-People trips in China and Cuba. These international experiences give her a personal understanding of the importance of diversity and cooperative living in our multi-cultural society, and allow her to present information that is critically important for individuals and the companies and organizations they represent. Sandra is also dedicated to her community, volunteering in the efforts to eliminate domestic violence, empower its victims and educate our youth. That dedication, coupled with her passion for professional development, allows her to provide dynamic, challenging, and thought-provoking seminars and workshops. She is certified by the American Heart Association as an instructor, Inscape Product instructor, National Safety Council instructor, OSHA instructor, Outreach trainer for Pinellas Technical Education Center (PTEC), a Professional Women's Network instructor, and a Safe Sitter instructor. Well, Sandra, you're tied up in all kinds of things. Welcome to our program today.

Sandra Contreras (Contreras)
Thank you.

Wright
Sandra, you've worked in several different industries and numerous jobs, and you've stated that you have knowledge on several subjects. How can you call yourself an expert in any field?

Contreras
I think if you really look at what I do, you will see that they are all connected by one common element: people. Working with people, talking to people and understanding how they connect with information is at the heart of what I do. When I am working with adults and/or children and aiming to teach them something such as CPR, for example, the goal is not only to instruct them on the technique, but to also leave them with a feeling of empowerment, knowing that they possess the skills to save someone's life. When I'm doing a workshop regarding professional development, it's basically the same thing. My goal is to coach them on the best way to present themselves to the public, while also instilling a sense of empowerment and increasing their self-esteem. It's the same type of thought process.

Wright
I've never heard of the Safe Sitter. What is that all about?

Contreras
The program was started in Indianapolis by a doctor whose colleague lost a child when her adult sitter was unable to perform the Heimlich maneuver on the choking child. Recognizing the need to equip caretakers with the knowledge of the various life-saving techniques, this doctor started the Safe Sitter program. I feel it's a wonderful program. I particularly like the program because it gives an emphasis on babysitting as a business. It not only instructs the young woman or young man—they do have young men who like to take the class—on the safety of the child, but it also talks about the safety of the sitters themselves. In my own experiences as a young woman act-

ing in the capacity of a sitter, there were several situations that I had gotten myself into where I would have benefited from the information that I teach my young students.

Wright

Well, that ought to make the parents feel better.

Contreras

Well, I think that anyone who hires someone with a Safe Sitter certification would feel more at ease leaving their children with them, especially in today's times. When they have completed the program, they receive a card that designates them as a Safe Sitter.

Wright

Sandra, you've lived and traveled extensively around the world. How has that affected the way you think and live?

Contreras

It affects me in the sense that I look at people and I don't see their exteriors. I look at their interior: who they are, what they have to say, where they've come from. I have found that with many of the people I talk to, other people would look at their exterior and assume that they are an uneducated person. These individuals tend to put a different emphasis on things than I do. When I approach people, I enjoy getting them to open up and tell me about themselves. You learn a lot of interesting things about people. For instance, I find that many of the people I meet speak more languages than I do, and I speak English and Spanish. I met one person who speaks Russian, German, Spanish, and some dialects of Arabic, and I'm going, "Wow! I can only speak two languages." My experiences abroad make me look beyond the frivolous things that other people consider important, such as cars and houses and other material possessions, and look beyond the surface to the person within.

Wright

Do you think that language is one of the most, or at least one of the top two or three things that keep us apart?

Contreras

No, I don't. What honestly keeps us apart is people are unwilling to share ideas, unwilling to talk to different people, and unwilling to see diversity as a blessing. I have met many people that would look at someone who wasn't dressed as appropriately or as well as they were and discount them as a person they would talk to. I don't think language stops us. I think it's our failure to be open to new ideas and new people.

Wright

I've heard you say that diversity is the spice of life. Can you tell our readers what you mean?

Contreras

I think that in order for us to grow and become better people, we have to challenge ourselves. Diversity, whether it applies to the people you interact with or the situations that you encounter, is a catalyst for change and growth. For example, I'm not particularly fond of horses, but I've been horseback riding in an effort to expand my horizons and enrich my life experiences. You would be surprised to find that it's these types of experiences they provide a starting point for some great conversations. Discovering the little things that you have in common with other people facilitates interaction and provides an opportunity to enrich your life thought processes. These diverse experiences provide a common ground with others and leads to many interesting discussions. As we touched on earlier, I find that learning other languages allows you to converse with people about their culture and their life. This exposure to something outside of your normal path affords you with an opportunity for personal growth.

Wright

Diversity for many years just simply meant the separation of black and white.

Contreras

Yes.

Wright

That is really unfortunate. In our church, we have a ministry in Mexico and I have learned just by being involved in that about the country and more about its people in the last two or three years than I have in all of my life.

Contreras

Well, that's a compliment to you because that's an opportunity to open up and be different. I'm sure if you had mentioned that to certain groups of people, they would look at you like you had lost your mind. Simply because, to them, it is something that's different and uncomfortable and they don't want to deal with it. I think we could learn a lot from looking at our children—they are like little sponges, they accept differences and they readily work with them.

Wright

Let me ask you a question. Do you consider yourself to be successful?

Contreras

I consider myself successful in the sense that I have accomplished many goals. There are many things I would like to continue to do, but I have raised a beautiful family. My daughters are all very functioning adults. They've graduated from school, and I consider my success more in those terms. I consider myself successful when I complete a class, and I see that the participants have caught on to a concept or have been exposed to material and information that is going to stimulate introspection. That is what success is to me. I'm working with a program right now where I teach social and vocational skills to individuals who speak English as a second language. When I see them catch on to something or see them repeat a word that was giving them difficulty, I view those occasions as successes that are important to me.

Wright

So, completions of goals or completions of tasks would be closer to your definition of success than anything else?

Contreras

Yes. I think that people view success in terms of the number of books they've sold, or the number of dollars that they have in their pocket. While those things are important as a means of supporting yourself, to me, they are not the ultimate measure of your life or your achievements.

Wright

What about happiness and enjoyment of life and those kinds of things, will they figure in success or are they just accoutrements that come through completing tasks?

Contreras

I think that people define happiness in many different ways. Personally, I define happiness as enjoyment of my family, my friends, and seeing the joy that I give to others. For some people, happiness is having a large bank account or simply fishing off the dock, enjoying the breeze. I think that people have to define happiness in their own terms. This is where diversity plays a key role—happiness for you, for me, for five other people down the road is not going to mean the same thing.

Wright

If you had to narrow it down, what is the one thing in your personal life that has contributed to your success?

Contreras

My daughters. They have given me the strength to get through some tough times and to continue moving forward. My life has taken several twists and turns over the years, and they have been there for me. Over the years, particularly during our tough times, they would say to me, "You know, Mom, you can do it. You told us we can do it." I think that is a great measure of success—knowing that you have people there to encourage and support you. When my daughters offer their words of encouragement, I look at them and realize that I instilled those thought processes in them.

Wright

You say they are both grown now?

Contreras

Yes.

Wright

My oldest son, I really spent a lot of time with him the entire time he was growing up, and fulfilling my life in those kinds of ways. Now that he is grown, I find that he is probably my best adviser and friend as well. Did that happen to you?

Contreras

Actually it did, David. I raised my two youngest daughters to be independent thinkers. I say my two youngest daughters because I have five, three of which are stepdaughters. I raised them the way that I would have liked to have been raised. I was raised in a time when women were seen but not heard. I wanted my daughters to feel that the sky was the limit, that they could do anything they wanted to do. My only wish for them was that they were happy and chose a path in life that would satisfy them. I think that, as you said, when you spend time with your children and you work with them, you sit back and reap the rewards of being able to ask for their advice. My children are very honest with me. When I ask them a question, I get an unbiased opinion. To me, that is very valuable. When you ask somebody for their opinion, you can either feel that they're giving you the truth or that they're telling you what they think you want to hear. When I ask my daughters, I know they're telling me what I need to hear, not necessarily what I want to hear. I think that's an extremely valuable asset. I wouldn't trade it for the world.

Wright

Sandra, with our book, we're trying to encourage our readers to be better, to live better, and be more fulfilled by listening to the examples of our guests. Is there anything or anyone in your life that has made a difference for you and helped you to become a better person?

Contreras

My father. He was the type of person who accepted people for what they were, without thinking about how he could change them or what he might like them to be. He never treated anybody rudely or unkindly. He was always very straightforward and honest. When I stray from my path sometimes, I think of the words that he always told us, "We should be very honest with people and remember that people may be lonely or in need of assistance. Sometimes a kind word will make a difference." So, I have always gone back to that thought process. I think it has worked very well for me.

Wright

What do you think makes up a great mentor? Someone like your father? In other words are there characteristics that mentors seem to have in common?

Contreras

I was asked to do a program on mentoring quite a few years ago with a women's group. It partnered older women with younger women to complete these picture puzzles, where you have pictures and letters and they make up a particular phrase or word. It was interesting that the older women suddenly became the mentee and the younger person became the mentor. To me, I think everyone in every situation is in a mentoring or mentor situation. You can listen to anyone and learn something from them. The ability to share is a characteristic of mentors, and most importantly, the ability to listen—truly listen—when somebody speaks.

Wright

When you consider the decisions that you have made down through the years, has faith played an important role in your life?

Contreras

Most definitely. With the death of my husband, it changed my entire life. He died about 14 years ago. We were in the process of leaving the States again moving to Spain, and all of a sudden my entire life was changed. I had to rethink my whole process. It was an eye opener.

Wright

And you had three of his children.

Contreras

They were older and they had already moved away. I had my two youngest children. We had basically closed up our house and had our furniture packed. It was on the dock ready to be shipped to Spain. My children had been taken out of school and were getting ready to be put into school in Barcelona. My husband died during a medical procedure, and it was a huge shock for my family. Now, when I talk to people, I try to be very empathetic, because I know how one missed step can change somebody's life forever.

Wright

So, the family was getting ready to move to Spain, to do what?

Contreras

My husband was going to be working on some hotels for the World Olympics in '92 and we were moving in '89.

Wright

So, all of a sudden, you find yourself alone with two young girls.

Contreras

Yes. Two young girls, a lot of family changes and a lot of life changes. My whole thought processes of what I wanted to do with my life had to change. I think I'm still going through those changes.

Wright

I'm not sure that's not a good thing.

Contreras

Well, actually, David, I think that we look at it as a good thing. My daughters and I have discussed it many times over the years, and their lives would have been totally different. This may not have been a bad thing, but the way their lives have turned out now, we look at it as a positive issue. I look at it as a positive opportunity for me to change. Otherwise, I'd be sitting every day in my bedroom rolled up in a fetal position, crying, and one of the things that keeps me going is knowing that alternative. Moving forward, moving on with my life, offering people an opportunity and information that will give them something to move forward with is a very positive thing.

Wright

If you could have a platform and advise our readers, what would you say to them regarding success?

Contreras

Most importantly, listen to yourself and trust in your own instincts and beliefs. But don't discount the advice of people that don't always agree with you. Many times we have the knowledge within ourselves, but are consumed with self-doubt. We do not take that step outside ourselves because of our fear—fear of success, fear of failure, fear that someone is going to laugh at us, or fear that we are going to lose money. All these fears come into play when we look at opportunities for success. At this time when we're most vulnerable, we may fall into the trap of listening to those people who tell us, "No, you can't do that." I don't believe in telling anybody that they can't do anything they want to do. If you want to do something, there's a way to do it, even though it may not be the "conventional" approach. My daughter has a learning difference, and so we had to approach her studies differently while she was in high school and college. But did it keep her from graduating and achieving her goals? No. We just had to find a different way to support her.

Wright

It's strange to hear you say a fear of success. It's almost a senseless statement when you think about it, but I agree with you. In my life at least, I've found that there are about as many people afraid of success as there are people afraid of failure.

Contreras

Failure is comfortable. With failure you don't have to grow. You can sit there and say, "Oh, I tried it and it didn't work." Well, you didn't try hard enough. You could have kept on going and would have been successful.

Wright

I heard someone say recently that 98 percent of all failure is due to quitting.

Contreras

Yes. Something as simple as picking up the phone and making that call, or having that one conversation with someone could change your entire life. I often think of our early inventors, like Thomas Edison and Alexander Graham Bell. They experienced failure, but believed strongly enough in themselves and their ideas to persevere. Likewise, I reflect on our Founding Fathers and the obstacles that they faced. I'm sure there were times when they wanted to just give up, but they didn't. Imagine what our world would be like if these individuals didn't possess such great courage.

Wright

Well, what an interesting conversation, and I really appreciate you spending this much time with me.

Contreras

Well, thank you, David. I appreciate the opportunity.

Wright

Today we have been talking to Sandra Contreras. She, as we have found through her working with various industries and various people, has learned a lot about what makes people tick. I really appreciate some of the things that you've helped me with today, Sandra. And I hope to talk to you again soon.

Contreras

Thank you, David, and thank you for sharing with me as well.

About The Author

Sandra Contreras has worked within a variety of industries, including construction, manufacturing and health care. She has owned and operated a successful tax service, worked in the real estate industry and for companies of various sizes in their accounting and personnel departments. Her professional experiences, combined with wit and wisdom have made her a popular speaker in seminars and workshops throughout the business community.

Sandra Contreras

Contreras Consulting

PO Box 22305

St. Petersburg, Florida 33742

Phone: 727.235.2272

Email: consultcontreras@aol.com

Website: www.contrerasconsulting.com

Chapter 7

KENDALL C. WRIGHT

David E. Wright (Wright)

As President and founder of Entelechy Training and Development, Inc., an organization dedicated to the actualization of human potential, Kendall C. Wright is swiftly becoming one of the most insightful authors and innovative speakers in the areas of motivation, management, and success. Kendall holds degrees in psychology, sociology and communications and an advanced degree in human resource development. In his career, Kendall has worked with many of the Fortune 500 companies as an expert trainer, consultant, and facilitator. For his hard work and contributions, Kendall has received many awards and honors to include: Listings in Outstanding Young Men of America, International Who's Who of Professionals, and the National Speakers Association Directory of Professional Speakers. Kendall is active in his community and serves as an associate minister at the United Missionary Baptist Church in Middletown, Ohio. Kendall speaks and conducts workshops at conventions, churches, and corporations on professional and personal development. Mr. Wright, welcome to *Conversations on Success.*

Kendall C. Wright (K. Wright)

Thank you, David. It's a pleasure to be with you.

Wright

Kendall, your company's name is very unique. What does it mean and is there a story there?

K. Wright

Oh, David, there is definitely a story there. I recall in the very early stages of defining the type of services the company would provide. I wanted to find the perfect word or phrase to embody the philosophy of the company. I wanted the perfect name that would be both encouraging and prophetic. One evening I was scanning the dictionary, that's the unabridged dictionary, looking at various words, just brainstorming. It had gotten pretty late and I hadn't found anything that really "spoke" to me. I put the dictionary back on the shelf above my desk. As I took my hand away, the book, literally, flipped off the shelf and landed open on my desk. As I looked over the page my eye fell upon a rather unusual and odd-looking word. I read the definition and began to "shout" right there. Entelechy, pronounced (En·tel'·ah·key), is a Greek derivative and it means the real existence of a thing, not merely its theoretical existence.

The second definition was equally as powerful, it referenced that in some cultures, entelechy is thought of as the life giving force believed to be responsible for the development of all living things. That was it. I often say it was given to me from above. So that's how Entelechy came to be the name of my company. I paraphrase all of that by saying Entelechy represents moving from possibility to reality.

Wright

What is the mission statement for Entelechy?

K. Wright

Because I'm so passionate about the work I do and the reaction that audiences have to keynotes and workshops, I have moved away from a "mission statement" to what I call a "passion statement." The passion statement for Entelechy is that I want to be an instrument of my Creator. I want to touch the lives of others sharing hope, self-development, self-respect, and optimism, all the while changing possibilities to realities.

Wright

How did you come up with the idea for your first book?

K. Wright

David, really, that was more by request than anything else. Over the years, as a part of my presentation style, I developed the practice of sharing what I call "Kendall-isms." These were one-liners or short poems I would use to highlight a point or key concept. People would often ask, "Do you have that written down?" or "Do you have that on a tape?" After several years of accumulating notes and insights, I finally decided to go ahead and organize them and share that information. The first project, which is called *Affirming and Confirming SuccessFUL™ Living—How to Cultivate a SuccessFUL™ Perspective,* has been a true blessing and extremely well received. It's been exhilarating and humbling to be a part of helping people gain a more optimistic approach to the challenges of life.

Wright

Affirming and confirming?

K. Wright

That's right affirming and confirming. You see, there's an impressive body of research around the power of affirmations, but you don't find as much literature on the confirmation of what has been affirmed. My insight or revelation came when I realized that it is the actual confirmation that empowers us to move on to do even bigger and better things.

Wright

Who or what does the confirming?

K. Wright

The learner, the reader, the participant in the journey of life. You. You confirm it through the daily experiences of your life. Each day you look for ways to prove to yourself that, yes, you are smart. Yes, you are talented. Yes, you have abilities that you didn't know you had. So daily you jot down a brief note as evidence of the "Fulness" of your life. And in doing so you create a "success record." By looking over your success record, you are empowered to go out and take the next risk. Taking on that next risk will lead to your next reward.

Wright

Tell us about you're A.C.T. model.

K. Wright

That's a great model. It is basically a three-step action plan or a framework. It's really a call for attention, a call to action, and a call to achievement. The letters, by their sequencing, tell us that we must act. We must take action to live the SuccessFUL™ life. A.C.T. is a powerful acronym for **A**spire, **C**ultivate, and **T**est. The story on how Entelechy Training and Development came into existence is nothing less than the A.C.T. model in action. Would you like to hear about that?

Wright

Sure.

K. Wright

Let's start with the call for attention. For years I aspired to be a motivational speaker. I found myself in the role of facilitator and trainer and as I received feedback at the end of each presentation people would tell me, "You're really good at this. You have a way of motivating people. You have the right package, personality, voice, and experience." So, for years I aspired, but I put forth no real action to make it a reality. Remember, work without a plan yields similar results as a plan with no work—sub optimum. So, I'm aspiring all over the place. I jotted down a note here or captured a concept there or created a model over there, but the effort was erratic. Finally after reflecting on the words of encouragement from many, many sources, I finally decided to put it together. It was time to put some perspiration together with all of this aspiration. At this point I began to head the call to action.

So, I worked many, many hours pouring over my notes, building concepts, reading books, listening to tapes, and after a while my own projects started to take shape. I was really overwhelmed by the volume of material that came pouring out of me. I found myself impressed and surprised by notes I had made over the years. As a matter of fact, I would read some of them and say, "Did I do this?" I purchased a small digital recorder and became serious about A.C.T., Aspire, Cultivate, and Test. I would record snippets and then test them. I would play sound bites for people at work. I would play them for people at church and friends. I became bold enough to even stop strangers in the mall. I would ask, "Listen to this and tell me what you think?" I would use their feedback to edit or modify the concept or its presentation, and then I would test it again. The resulting reality is now I am enjoying the call to achievement. Literally, Aspire, Cultivate, and Test is the model that allowed me to be with you today.

Wright

What is SuccessFUL™ living and in that question, you spell it success and then you capitalize the FUL. It's a trademark isn't it?

K. Wright

It is. It is, indeed. I was looking for a way to capture the full essence of life. I believe everyone wants to live a full and successful life. So looking at successful and playing on the word, I created a simple graphic representation of the concept. That led to my trademarking the SuccessFUL™ with the FUL capitalized and underlined. The graphic and concept are intended to be instrumental in helping us to understand that SuccessFUL™ living is not marked by accumulation but by aspiration. That is an aspiration to actualize the amazing potential within each of us. SuccessFUL™ living is not marked by stagnation, but by cultivation—that is the cultivation of knowledge, insights, skills and abilities. SuccessFUL™ living is not marked by timidity, but by testing—that is testing the illusions of limits, lack and less than. So, the concept is one of empowerment and getting outside of our comfort zone.

Wright

How do you calibrate success? I've heard success defined probably as many times as I've heard speakers try to define it. What does it mean to you?

K. Wright

People are truly SuccessFUL™ when they are working toward the fulfillment of their individual potential. The way I often illustrate success is through the use of a life scenario. If just one year ago I had been hit by a Metro bus and my legs were crushed and mangled, but yet today, I'm in the Cincinnati Flying Pig Marathon and it takes me 26 hours to complete the course, am I successful? No doubt I am because that accomplishment is evaluated or viewed in direct proportion to the ability I have at that moment. Now someone else may complete that marathon in 2 hours and 28 minutes. To compare myself against that person only sets me up for disappointment. So, for me, success is looking at the ability you have now and actualizing that ability and potential.

Wright

Can you expound on this original idea that you have called "Motive-bration."

K. Wright

That is a great one. "Motive-bration" is a term I coined as I was searching for the perfect combination of motive and celebration. It was my observation that there was a powerful interplay between motive and celebration. Motive being, of course, that which drives us, and celebration refers to the activity of rejoicing. What I've noticed is that those persons who are truly SuccessFUL™ celebrate their reason or their purpose for contributing—contributing to others, contributing to the society, contributing to the neighborhood. It was clear that having a reason to act is what excites the truly SuccessFUL™.

So, for me, when I think about celebrating and having a reason to celebrate, I asked, what are some of the things people enjoy celebrating? We celebrate birthdays, promotions, holidays and accomplishments. Well, correspondingly, a motive-bration is the celebration of the birth of a reason. Motive-bration is the promotion of your potential. Motive-bration is a permanent holiday from mediocrity. So, motive-bration is again, a celebration of aspiring, cultivating, and testing. If you don't have a reason to act, you won't. That's why it's so important to understand that motive is what drives us to the next level of performance or accomplishment.

Wright

So, from the get-go you're saying that the celebration begins when the idea begins and the goal is set.

K. Wright

Well said, David, because, again, if you don't have a reason to take the action, it won't happen. It won't happen.

Wright

What's your understanding of fear and its impact on achievement?

K. Wright

Fear can be a powerful and debilitating emotion. In my keynotes and workshops I've tried to share how to manage and master "fear" in order to see our potential come to fruition. Of course, you're probably familiar with the old acronym that *Zig* made popular that fear is false evidence appearing real. I have a couple of my own. Fear is what results when **f**ailure is **e**levated **a**bove **r**eality. Fear is what we get when we become preoccupied with **f**uture **e**valuation **a**nd **r**ejection. Fear is the smog that allows the **f**amiliar to **e**clipse the **a**dventure and **r**ewards.

Fear could be thought of and described through the use of, perhaps, countless allegories. Three that I have found to be useful are fear as an antacid, fear as a sponge, and fear as curare. Curare is a poison made from the South American Strawberry Dart Frog. Let's just look at fear as an antacid. Just as Rolaids neutralize the acids of our digestive system, fear neutralizes the power of our essence, the power of our being. Fear acts as an antacid to our potential. One or two tablets of fear can literally rob you of your will. It can rob you of your ability to take action. Very often the things we fear most are the very things we create in our lives. Remember, that on which we meditate, we create. For example, if I'm fearful of my wife leaving me for another man. I will begin to fixate on that possibility. I will become so preoccupied with that thought that I begin to see things as if they were. I start to project my inner thoughts on my outer world. My suspicions rise and I begin to distance myself from her, question her and spy on her. Now, you know she can sense this mistrust and distance, wouldn't you think?

Wright

Of course.

K. Wright

How then will she react to the situation? Remember, you get what you give. So, she starts to give me "some of me." Of course, I don't like that and it further fuels my fire, and the vicious cycle continues. In the end, I have created the very thing I feared. Ultimately she leaves, and I say, "I told you so." What we fear most, we very often create.

Wright

Do you offer any insight or methodology as to how to overcome fear?

K. Wright

David, the first thing to do in overcoming fear is to face the fear. Just acknowledge that it is there. Then educate yourself on the whys and whats around that particular situation. Then you have to take action. You have to step into it. Remember the book, *Feel the Fear and Do It Anyway*; there is great truth in that statement. So, face it and take the action to move through it and when you do so, you can reclaim whatever it is that fear has stolen from you. David, isn't it amazing how we have been duped by fear? Fear has actually mounted one of the most sophisticated recruitment programs ever known to mankind. You may not know this, but many of us are working with our fears versus fighting our fears. We've become unwitting accomplices to our own underachievement, frustration, and stagnation.

Wright

I had a minister one time go to the blackboard. You're familiar with the equal sign with a slash through it? Which means it is not equal to.

K. Wright

That's right.

Wright

He wrote fear on the left-hand side and knowledge on the right hand side. Down through the years I have tried to let that be at least a partial guide to me.

K. Wright

Know that fear is faith working in reverse. So, that's, again, just another way that fear controls us by making us unwitting accomplices. Fear gets us into an unsuspecting alliance that actually brings about our own defeat.

Wright

How does motivation fit in today's workplace?

K. Wright

That is a great question. I think, motivation has a role in the workplace, but I think it starts with managers. You see, in order for managers to be effective motivators, there are a couple of distinctions that must be understood. If management is, by definition, getting things done through other people, then having those others operate in a "state of motivation" is in the best interest of all concerned. Motivation, however, has been mistakenly confused with excitation and animation. Motive is finding and having a reason to take action. So, managers can help motivate employees by practicing five simple principles.

Number one, they have to share the big picture. When people are more fully informed as to how their contribution fits into the larger picture, they can feel a sense of pride and ownership in the final product. Number two, managers have to share their faith and belief in the team. The classic psychological model of the Pygmalion Effect has been proven time and time again to have a measurable impact on employees and performance. The manager who shares his or her genuine belief and confidence in the team's ability to actualize the goals will position that team for a win. Number three, the manager has to share clear expectations and objectives. A double-minded man can never plow a straight furrow. Few things can diffuse a "can-do attitude" as quickly as confusion. The employees need to have a sense of where they're going and why. Number four is that the motivating manager has to share frequent feedback, whether it is positive or negative. Feedback can serve as a significant motivator to behavioral modification. Lastly, the motivating manager has to share the credit. Sharing the credit goes a long way in motivating the staff. What could be more inconsistent than to talk about T.E.A.M., Together Everyone Achieves More, yet the manager's behaviors suggest they're thinking every accomplish is management's. The motivating manager is an indispensable asset to the 21st century organization.

Wright

You draw an interesting distinction between training and education. Could you expand that a little bit for us?

K. Wright

Yes, David. Too often I find that organizations are attempting to educate the hand and train the head. But that won't work. It can't work. You see, when people are looking for whys, they're looking for education. When they are looking for hows, they are looking for training. Organizations should remember that we have to train the hand and educate the head.

Wright

That is very interesting. What area most needs leadership development today?

K. Wright

That's a tough question David, in the sense of its magnitude. The answer is leadership is needed from the CEO's office all the way out to the curb of the street. It's needed all the way from the pulpit to the front door of the church and all places and spaces in between. Previous thinking that leadership was somehow reserved for the elite few, or the talented tenth, led to our current situation today—where it's hard to find effective leadership, and the concept of servant-based leadership is practically non-existent, even in many churches. That's because we're not growing leaders. We're growing followers. True leaders grow leaders. Insecure leaders grow followers.

Wright

Someone told me in an interview recently that the difference between management and leadership was vision. Do you agree with that?

K. Wright

I agree. I think that the leader's responsibility is to sell the story, to share the vision with the troops, if you will. The managers take care of the how-to's.

Wright

You have developed an incredible paradigm that you refer to as the E.L.M. tree. Could you share the basics of that paradigm?

K. Wright

William Blake, the celebrated British poet, offered, "A fool sees not the same tree that the wise man sees." As we aspire, cultivate, and test to achieve, become and to obtain all of what life has to offer, we must be ever mindful of the symbolism of the elm tree. The three letters that make up the name elm are emblematic of Ethical, Legal, and Moral. The E epitomizes Ethical, L is the link to Legal, and M alerts us to Morals. The E.L.M. is essential to enjoying the Success-FUL™ life. Ethical is defined by the governance of your profession or your trade. Legal is defined by the laws of the land. Moral is defined by the divine code. David, keeping the E.L.M. in mind will help us steer clear of the most enticing temptation in all professions. That temptation is to compromise our integrity. Compromised integrity is corrupted success.

Wright

As I've been listening to you talk, you haven't mentioned the word, but I've heard it in so much of your intonation in your sentences and that word would be character. It must be a really important thing for you in your success models.

K. Wright

I was speaking with one of my colleagues earlier today and he remarked that image is only gold plating, but character is 24-karat gold. There is just no substitute for character. Consider this, David, success gained via unscrupulous avenues cannot be enjoyed with respect and particularly cannot be enjoyed with self-respect. Externally, we may put forward a façade of self-assuredness and respectability and integrity, but the incongruity of our thoughts, speech and behavior can, and may, become maddening. In time, the veneer wears thin. In the still of the night when we're alone, the guilty conscience will remind us of the shame and disgrace associated with how we "earned" the advancement or assignment or accomplishment. Is there any joy in getting an A for which you cheated? Is there any pride in gaining a seat in an election that you riddled with fraud and fabrication and forgery? Is there any real peace in conning others or yourself? Using the E.L.M. model as the standard, the answer to each of those questions must be a deafening no!

Wright

Having watched our country grow for six decades, I often wonder when I look back and read about men of great power and great wealth from presidents to CEOs and see how much we have attained through these people as our leaders. I always wonder where we would be had they really been men and women of character?

K. Wright

What I try to remind myself of daily and to share with my audiences is disregarding the principles of the E.L.M. predisposes us to remorse, regret, and self-resentment. There is nothing quite like the comfort of a good shade tree. So, if we stay in the shade of the E.L.M.

tree, we'll be protected from the heat of disgrace, disbarment, re-scinded licenses and embarrassment.

Wright

What is most gratifying about the work that you do presently?

K. Wright

I really enjoy playing a small part in people taking that step of faith to really tap into their full potential. When they send notes or call or they come up after a keynote and they have tears in their eyes and they say something like, "You touched me. You gave me the reason I've been looking for to take my next step." There is nothing as gratifying as helping someone step into their full potential. Additionally, I must say, watching my own growth has been extremely inspiring. Thirty-five years ago, there was no way I would have seen myself doing the things I am doing now. It's exciting!

Wright

What an interesting conversation and I really do appreciate you being a part of this conversation and this book. It has really taught me a lot today.

K. Wright

David, I'm glad to have the opportunity. Continue to Aspire, Cultivate, and Test and God will take care of the rest!

Wright

We have been talking today to Kendall C. Wright who is becoming one of the most insightful authors and innovative speakers in the areas of motivation, management, and success. We really appreciate you sharing your views with us today.

K. Wright

You're welcome.

About The Author

Commanding, Dynamic and Motivating. These are just a few of the terms audiences of all types have used to describe the presence, personality, and power that Kendall C. Wright brings to the platform. Wright is swiftly becoming one of the most insightful authors and innovative speakers in the areas of Leadership, Motivation and Success. With a Bachelor's degree in Psychology, a Master's degree in Human Resource Development, and more than two decades of experience, Kendall has instructed, enlightened, and empowered thousands of students, managers, and leaders.

Kendall C. Wright
PO Box 1515
West Chester, Ohio 45071-1515
Phone, Fax: 513.860.4934
Email: Kendall@EntelechyCan.com
Website: www.EntelechyCan.com

Chapter 8

RUSSELL J. WHITE

THE INTERVIEW

David E. Wright (Wright)

Today we're talking to Russell J. White, President of Russell J. White International, Inc. He is an international speaker, a corporate trainer, a management consultant and author. Drawing on his more than 20 years of experience as a Fortune 500 manager and consultant, he combines visionary, innovative approaches for positioning organizations for the future with straight-forward, practical strategies for meeting tomorrow's challenges today. He was named Businessperson of the Year in recognition of his professional success and community involvement. He is a member of the National Speaker's Association, past chairman of NSA's Motivational Professionals Group, and President-elect of NSA Carolinas. Mr. White, welcome to *Conversations on Success.*

Russell J. White (White)

Thank you.

Wright

One of your latest books is entitled *Little White Truths: Lessons for Leadership*. I've heard of little white lies, but what are little white truths?

White

Well, the little white truths are the counter to the little white lies that are so prevalent in way too many business organizations today. Honestly, I think I made an underestimation when I titled that book. I think I should have called them big white truths, because in the last few years we've seen how much power they have to transform lives. Big white truths are the realities of success. One, for example, would be "champions possess a clarity of focus." When I work with athletes or I work with champion businesspeople, I find that they have this tremendous focus on whatever task they're trying to accomplish. They have a clearly defined measure of success, what they want to achieve, and their entire lives are just focused on that point.

Another big white truth would be "you impact people with every encounter." I think so many people miss an opportunity to have tremendous impact and to create success in another person's life because they take these minor encounters for granted. I find out that even something as slight as getting on an elevator with someone and saying, "You look really nice today," and truly meaning it makes a difference. What that person does when they leave the elevator and how you impacted them can have a tremendous benefit. Now those are just little things.

I find out that people who are true leaders are always looking for ways to have a positive impact on other people and not look for the negative opportunity that we see so much on television—the funny get-back or the way to get on top of someone else and try to squash them down. I just see big white truths as looking for the positive impact.

"Success is servanthood" is another big white truth. I think people who are very, very successful are good at serving whomever it is that they need to be serving. That's also what creates leadership for them. I would say another big white truth that I've experienced and that I've seen tremendously through a lot of organizations and successful people is "when you believe in the possible, sometimes the impossible will happen."

Wright

When I read the title, I thought, without having read the book, I thought it had to do with character issues.

White

A lot of that is, as far as you impact people with every encounter. Your character comes out when you talk to people that you've never met before or that are—I hate to use the word—insignificant in your life, but just that chance encounter, how you treat people is really what comes out of your character. Do you cut them off in traffic? If they're asking for directions, do you just tell them, "I don't know and leave me be?" Or are you there to help people out? Are you there to help them get along their way a little bit better? I have seen that done with many successful managers that truly carry the leadership title with them because they take the time to look at the new employees and say, "I want to help you be successful. I want to sit down with you and really share with you my philosophy on what it takes to be successful in this business." By taking that kind of time, they don't get that much of a return on their investment of their time, as busy as they are, but they get their return by their investment in other people.

Wright

You know, I have been working with, listening to, or dealing in some way with the speaking industry and speakers in particular since about the early 70s. Gosh, I've seen topics come and go and important topics and buzzwords and all like that, but I have never experienced such a wave of discussions about character. Has it come to that? That we have to tell people that they should have good character? What is that all about?

White

Well, I tell you, all you have to do is look at the newspapers. Basically the police report is now the business page.

Wright

Isn't that something?

White

It's a shame that it has come to that. What's funny is that years ago when the Enron situation came out, I thought, okay, here's the wakeup call for everyone. They're going to see this and make that the unfortunate model not to fall into and then they'll clean up their act because of that. But obviously, with what we're seeing today, that hasn't been happening. People are looking at the Enron thing and saying, "Oh, well, they made the mistake because they got caught," not, "I should change my behavior."

Honestly, I think a lot of that is because people misdirected their success. When your success is measured by profits and pure stockholder wealth at the expense of almost everything else, I think your direction is off and your character is off. I think that's why we have to regain our focus. If I'm focused on just money, just the bottom line, and what the market is doing everyday, I'm missing my customers, I'm missing my employees, I'm missing myself. Where's my truth to myself?

Wright

What do you see as the main obstacle people encounter in achieving success?

White

People fail to think big. What do I mean by that? Thinking big doesn't mean more money. It doesn't mean how big I can grow a company. It's thinking big as in "what could we do with the resources that we have? What is the long range view?" Thinking big is down the road. I think the main obstacles fall into two categories. A lot of people that I run into are people who suffer from what I call "yes, buts." When I talk to people and talk about thinking big, it seems so simple, why wouldn't everybody think big? I ask someone, "Do you want to think big?" and they say, "Yes, but success just isn't worth the price anymore." Or they say, "Yes, but I have car payments and a mortgage and two children to put through school, so it's the wrong time." Or they say, "My boss shoots down every idea I have." "Yes, but what if I fail?" "Yes, but I'm happy with where I'm at, so why rock the boat?" Those are the kinds of things that I hear people in the "yes, but" category saying. They fail to think big because of their most immediate obstacles that they see in front of them. I think there is another group of people as well who see things as impossible and therefore they don't even try.

Wright

Have you ever attempted anything that you considered impossible?

White

As a matter of fact, since I was writing all of these things in my last book about seeing the possible and the impossible might happen, I realized that I didn't have an example from my own life. So I asked myself about a year ago, "What is the most impossible thing that I could do with this body." I set my "impossible" goal to try to achieve crossing the finish line of a marathon upright, injury free, and not last. Those were my targets. For a 270 pound, 6 foot, 3 inch, 45-year-old man, that's a huge step. That was my impossible.

After six months of training and working with a team I went to Myrtle Beach, South Carolina, to run in the Bi-Lo Marathon down there. My slogan was "Run, Walk, and Crawl, I'll do 'em all." I completed the marathon; I crossed the finish line. A few people were there cheering for me. It was a tremendous accomplishment for me. I learned a lot of things along the way. I learned that the first 20 miles were what my training was there for. The last 6.2 miles was all mental because my body was telling me to quit on emotional, spiritual, physical, psychological levels—it was just saying stop. But it was the will to work through it. That was the only way I can describe how I got through the last 6.2 miles. Then I had a really neat giggle at the end of it when I crossed the finish line they hung a gold medal around my neck. I didn't know that everyone who crossed the finish line got the gold medal. I was in pretty good spirits, and I like to have fun with people, so I looked at the fellow and I said, "Well, what did I get a gold medal for?" He paused for a minute, thought and said, "Well, you did finish first in your weight class." So, that's me doing the impossible. I was able to complete the marathon, I'm very proud of the fact, and it's something that I will never forget. Not only did I accomplish something that day, but also it taught me the value of believing in the possible and the impossible does happen sometimes. I still—to this day—can't imagine how I did that, but I did. I believe if someone like me can do something like that, then I think it's within everybody's capability to do things that they think are impossible. They just haven't set the goal to do it or made the decision to make it happen. That's a matter of thinking big. I could have just said, "I'll do a half marathon," or "I'll do a 10K." But I wanted to think big. I wanted to go after the big idea with the realization that if I failed I would learn from that. It wouldn't be the end of the world. But I was so focused on completing it that I was able to do that.

Wright

I would say that after having passed the finish line that if I closed you up in a room right now and forced you to write about the experience and write only about those characteristics that caused you to finish that race, you'd probably develop a pretty good plan of success, wouldn't you?

White

Oh, no question. And I have to say I don't have a runner's body, I've never had any running experience at any time in my life. I've been semi-athletic in things that I've done, but that's a whole completely different type of experience. It was truly an emotional and mental win—for lack of a better word. The commitment, the dedication, the drive, the perseverance. I really believe that successful people have dedication, commitment, drive, perseverance and that's what makes them so successful.

Wright

You also talked about your team and you talked about the people on the sides cheering you on too.

White

This was not a one-person event. Everybody talks about a marathon as a singular event. But I never could have made it without my wife, number one, because at every five miles, she was there with Gatorade and a fresh pair of socks to minimize the blisters. Every five-mile point—he was there. So at 5, 10, 15, but when I got to mile 20 I had such severe blisters I didn't want to take my shoes off and look because I thought it would shut me down. So, we persevered through that.

I was a part of the Team in Training, which is a fund-raising group for the Leukemia and Lymphoma Society. They taught me how to train, what was the proper way to train, what was the proper footwear to have, and, of course, they had people there with me who helped me along through the training. So, it's truly surrounding yourself with good people.

We had some mind games that we played. There were three of us that were very close and moving at about the same pace. We agreed that none of us had ever done a marathon before and that, mentally, we just couldn't wrap our minds around a 26.2-mile marathon. So what we decided to do was five 5-mile runs and then a 1.2-mile victory lap. So, that was mentally how we achieved that. So, when we got to 15, we hadn't done 15 miles, we had just finished our third 5-miler and now we needed to do 5 more miles. That was how we motivated ourselves along. It was a game, but it worked for us. We alSo, decreed that there was no negativity allowed. Nobody could talk about how much they hurt. Nobody was allowed to talk about the pain they were in, because we were all in that pain, but we couldn't focus on the negative. We couldn't talk about the less than favorable weather; we couldn't talk about anything other than being very positive and upbeat. We enjoyed the homes as we went by, took notice of the crowd along the way, and appreciating some of their input. It was a matter of keeping everything very, very, very positive.

Wright

So, how does one learn to think big?

White

I think that there are seven strategies that enable you to think big. The first is to overcome your fear of failure. As simple as that sounds, I have been really surprised at how many people I've encountered in managerial ranks, in executive ranks, and all walks of life that are truly bound by a fear of failure. They're unable to see the benefit of learning through a failure. There's a quote that I use in one of my seminars that says, "Success isn't final and failure isn't fatal." Failure isn't fatal, so you've got to overcome the fear of failure first. The second thing is you've got to let your confidence soar. I looked around and saw a running club that was all dressed in the same uniform the morning of the marathon and I outweighed all of them, combined. It would have been real easy for my confidence to erode and say, "I'm just going to go back to IHOP and eat a stack of pancakes because that's what my body is made for." But I had to let my confidence just soar. I'm backtracking just a little bit, but a little thing happened at the starting line. There were 3,500 people there, it was pitch black because it was 6 o'clock in the morning, and a lady comes up to me and says, "You're Russell White." I said, "Son of a gun, you're right. Who are you?" She said, "You used to stay at my bed and breakfast in Charleston 7 years ago and I remember you." That was the one thing that made me think, "She remembered me. I'm important." I'm a big guy. I can think big, and boom it just let my confidence soar. It was just one of those magic moments that I needed to hear to eliminate any kernel of doubt that I may have had of "what in the heck did I get myself into?" So, that's the key, you've got to let your confidence soar.

The other thing is that if you look in the locker room before a big game, nobody is saying, "Oh my gosh, this other team is so good." Their confidence is saying, "We can beat anybody tonight." I think that's the second point.

The third point on thinking big is: Don't let small people get in the way of your big ideas. Small people are ones that want to knock you down, take credit for what you're trying to come up with, or the people who say, "We can't do this because." Don't let them shut you down. If you want to think big, you've got to figure out how to get past or get around those kinds of folks. All levels of hierarchy within an organization are filled with small people.

Fourth, start taking action. To become a Think BIG person requires more than just BIG ideas. It takes BIG action to put those big ideas in motion and it has to come from a discipline within. A Think BIG person doesn't wait for others to lead the way, doesn't wait for others to place expectations, and doesn't wait for a deadline to begin looming. A Think BIG person starts taking action to make the BIG ideas work.

Next, get rid of the box. The phrase "Thinking outside of the box" is so commonplace anymore that it's actually in-the-box thinking! Small thinkers want to only update the last strategic plan because it saves time and isn't really broken. They want to rely on well-worn excuses for reasons why goals aren't reached. Small thinkers like the box.

If you want to Think BIG you need to get wayward. You need to stimulate your creativity to reach new levels of thinking. When was the last time you spend meaningful time in thought about a situation at work? I'm not only talking about how to solve problems, or how to increase profits. I'm talking about thought with depth.

Sixth, constantly experiment. If you are going to think freely and Think BIG, then you have to experiment. After all, everything in life is experimentation. As children we are experimenting daily with learning how to ride a bike, how best to talk to a member of the opposite sex, taste new things we've never tasted before, allowing the senses to be alive! As adults we fall into routines because we have more to lose if we fail (or so we think). BIG Thinkers aren't afraid of taking bold steps to experiment and learn. Weigh the consequences, measure the risks, and continue the learning process by constant experimentation.

And seventh, and perhaps, most important, enjoy every step of the journey. So often we forget to enjoy the journey we are on. We get wrapped up in how we can afford this or that, or if we are ever going to see retirement. The pressures of life are tremendous to us and sometimes you might feel you are fighting just to keep your head about the water line. But, if you've ever traveled to a third-world country where daily health risks are real, and daily wages seldom purchase the necessities for living, you get a new perspective on how good we have it.

Wright

In your books and articles, you stress over and over that the successful managers are the ones who are leaders as well. How do you define leadership?

White

Being known as a manager comes with the position. That comes with your title. But being known as a leader comes from the willingness of others to follow you. I think the characteristics of a leader depend on the group of people that are following. For example, a coach has to have certain characteristics so that people want to be on your team. What is it that Coach K (Mike Krzyzewski) with the Duke University basketball team has that everybody wants to follow behind him? It's the relationship that he builds with his players. It's his successful nature. It's his focus on, not just winning, but everybody performing at their best and the wins will come. It's his caring for people. If you look at community leaders—why do we have community leaders? I don't just mean the people that are elected. What is it about them? They have a great concern—maybe it's for the roads of the community and they make a big impact on that. It's the characteristics they have of caring and coming back to that servanthood. One of the things that I think we're going to see a big change in is that leaders in the business world will be any executive that has earned the trust of people and values people and takes a long term view of his or her business. I see that as the trend of leadership that will be more desired from here on—especially with what we've gone through in American business in the last five, six, ten years.

Wright

Is leadership simply confined to the workplace? How is leadership manifested elsewhere?

White

Leadership is a mindset. It's not just, like I said, by title. I find that the people who are leaders in business are also the same people that are community leaders, leaders within schools, within their churches, and within their families. It's just a mindset of willingness to lead a group of people to achieve a particular benefit. I think that's the key. Leadership is more of an internal mentality and people just gravitate toward leaders. When they have this "success is servanthood" mentality, they're there to serve their constituents, their church members, their families, whomever, and it's not something they turn on and off when they go in and out of work. It's a characteristic as you said earlier. It's a personal characteristic of believing in something, wanting to make something happen, and serving and helping people to achieve their own success. I think that's the foundation for leaders.

Wright

What's leadership going to look like in the future? I hear managers talking about a new generation of employees with different values. Is that going to change how we lead successfully?

White

I think so. I think that we're going to see a tremendous backlash against the recent trends of maximizing wealth at all costs and there's going to be a greater concern for building—or in some cases rebuilding—trust in the workplace. I think the key in your question is values. I think people are going to come back to, "Is this a place I can work at and trust people? Is this a place that I can be comfortable in my relationships with people?" We used to refer to companies with poor working conditions as "sweatshops." Today, no one wants to be identified as a sweatshop, but the fact of the matter is—while we do not call them that—we do have what we call "churn and burn" organizations, which aren't much different than a sweatshop of yesteryear. I think that the values of the coming generation are more relationship oriented than profit oriented. I really see that that's going to be a huge change as we go through the new generations. Also, I'm finding out that I have a lot of managers who tell me they have a difficult time leading the new generation in the workforce. How do we make them comply? My recommendation is, you don't. You learn what their values are and lead them through their values. The fact of the matter is that coming generations are more interested in family than they are in work. Their priorities are shifting to family before work. For Baby Boomers, that's a big change. That's something that I think, personally, is a healthy move that we can have better balance and they're looking more for integrity than they are a 401(k).

Wright

It sounds like you see people's definition of success changing. This gets into more Gen-X type stuff.

White

It does. Absolutely. Our parents, the builder generation, defines success in growth and financial stability. They wanted to have it better than their parents did in the Depression. They wanted to grow communities and have good stability for retirement and for their kids. The Baby Boomer generation strives for personal recognition and achievement. We are very much interested in the "me" thing. We measure it by our own financial success. How big of a house can I get? How big of a salary can I get? What was my most successful year? When you ask a person of the Baby Boomer generation—not everybody, obviously we've got to be careful with generalities—but a lot of them, what was your most successful year, they're going to tell you the year they made the most money or made the best decision financially. Future generations are going to define success as having multiple experiences and building solid relationships. That's one of the things that is a big change for businesses because I really believe that the future generations aren't going to be profit-driven. Obviously they want to be profitable, but they're more interested in building good relationships and having lots of different experiences. I see people job-hopping, not necessarily for the money change, it's for the experience change. They want to work with their friends, which is a more healthy work environment in their minds. That's more important than how much money they make, as long as they can make ends meet. I think that's going to be a big change in the definition of success. Success is going to be defined by quality of life. Do I have a good time during my day or do I just crawl home, almost literally, at the end of the day dreading going back the next? I don't think that the coming generations are going to put up with that, whereas our generation has said they'd do that so long as the money was there.

Wright

I'd like to question one thing that we talked about.

White

Sure.

Wright

I have heard over the last ten years through all kinds of people, books, tapes, and trainers, that the difference between leadership and management is vision. Whereas I can understand that and partially agree with it, you brought something else to the table in your conversation a few minutes ago. I remember a man telling me many years ago, "David, if you think you're a leader and you look behind you and no one is following you, you're only out for a walk."

White

That's exactly right.

Wright

So, you've kind of put that in the mix now. So, you talk about managers being leaders and people elect to follow them. So, even though a manager by title may be carrying out the leader who has a vision by definition of his job, there is still that part down in him that can be a leader as well.

White

Oh, absolutely. It's really interesting to me. When I worked in textiles, before I got into this business almost a lifetime ago, I had 185 people working for me at one point. There was one gentleman that had been in the business for 45 years, and he was a mechanic. But he was the leader of the workforce. It didn't matter what I said. It didn't matter the direction that I gave. Everybody looked to him to see if he agreed with me or not. It didn't take long for me to realize that I had to earn his respect to get him on my side to make sure that I had the whole workforce with me. It was a real interesting thing because I was very young at the time and I expected as manager and department director that people should be following me. It didn't come with the title. I had to earn that. Being a young college boy only in the business a couple years, I hadn't earned that credibility yet like this gentleman had in the 45 years he had been in the business. That's when I learned a real valuable lesson that leadership is not about title, it's about people being willing to follow you.

You used a quote that I really liked about just being out for a walk. There was another quote that I liked that I've heard from other speakers that said, "managers do things right, but leaders do the right thing." It's one that I use repeatedly with some of my organizations. Sometimes the leader has to make the hard decision that's not popular, that's not fun, but that fits the vision and is the right thing to do whereas the manager might not do it for fear of being hurt in the short term. I think that's the difference. And I think that's a big difference. Leaders think big!

Wright

Well, what a great *Conversation on Success*. I really appreciate you being with us today. It's been very enlightening for me.

White

Great. I've enjoyed the opportunity to speak with you.

Wright

Today we have been talking to Russell J. White. He is the President of Russell J. White International, Inc. He is an international speaker, a corporate trainer, a management consultant, an author, and, as we have found out today, a very thoughtful leadership and management teacher. Thank you so much, Russell, for being with us.

White

Dave, it was a pleasure.

About The Author

The BIG Guy knows BIG is an attitude, not a size. As an informational speaker with a humorous style, he shows his audiences how to Think BIG and create a BIGGER future. His clients have him coming back year after year. He has written three books, his columns on leadership appear regularly in national magazines and business publications, and he has been selected Businessperson of the Year.

Russell J. White

Phone: 877.275.9468

Website: www.thinkBIGguy.com.

Chapter 9

NIDO QUBEIN

THE INTERVIEW

David E. Wright (Wright)

Today we are talking to Nido Qubein who is chairman of an international consulting firm and recipient of the highest awards given for professional speakers, including the Cavette which is known as the "Oscar" of professional speaking, the Speaker's Hall of Fame and sales and marketing, International's Ambassador of Free Enterprise. Toastmasters International named him the top business and commerce speaker and awarded him the Golden Gavel Medal. He served as president of the National Speakers Association which has a membership of a thousand professionals. Nido has been the recipient of many honors, including the Ellis Island Medal of Honor, a doctorate of laws degree and induction into Beta Gamma Sigma, the honor society for business leadership. Nido's business savvy lead him to help start a bank in 1986 and today he serves on the board and executive committee of a Fortune 500 financial corporation with 90 billion dollars in assets. He is also chairman of a National Public Relations Company and chairman of Great Harvest Bread Company with 200 stores in 38 states and chairman of the Miss North Carolina/Miss USA Program. He serves on the boards of 17 universities, companies and community organizations, including all three of his alma maters.

Nido has written numerous books and recorded scores of audio and video learning programs, including a best seller on effective communication published by Nightingale, Coenit and Berkley. He is an active speaker and consultant addressing more than 100 businesses and professional groups around the world each year. He doesn't just talk business, he lives it. He is an entrepreneur with active interests in real estate, advertising and banking. Nido Qubein, welcome to *Conversations on Success*.

Nido Qubein (Qubein)
Thank you very much, I'm glad to be here.

Wright
Nido, when you came to the United States as a teenager you could not speak English, you had no contacts and you had only $50.00 in your pocket. Today you are a multi-millionaire. Tell our readers how you felt when you arrived in the United States.

Qubein
I arrived in the United States with a heart full of expectation, a lot of hope, aspirations, desire to make something worthwhile come of my life and also a truckload of willingness to work hard and work smart and make good things come to be. You know people every year want to come to America because they know and they believe that this is a nation where those who are willing to pursue their dreams and willing to pay the price and pay their dues along the way can make something significant happen.

Wright
Some time ago you told me your father died when you were six years old. Who raised you and what impact did your father's death have on your early life?

Qubein
Sometimes, someone doing a story will ask if I could change one thing in my life what would that one thing be. I'm pretty clear on the answer to this question, I certainly would want to have a dad if I could change on thing. I would want to have a dad in my life because he did die when I was six and my mother brought us up. Five of us, three boys and two girls. My mother had fourth grade education and yet wiser than 25 Ph.D.'s from the finest Ivy League schools of your

own picking. And the reason really is that she has a post graduate degree in a disciple you would call common sense. Some would say she has common sense, it isn't as common as it once was. She taught me some of the greatest principles, some fundamentals, some of the most savvy advice about planting seeds for a better life and moving onwards and upwards with vigor and tenacity. She taught me things like this for example: Who you spend time with is who you become. So, if you want to be great, you've got to walk side by side, hand in hand with great people. She said it's not the circumstances in which you find yourself that define the person you become, it's the choices you make that define the person you become, so choose well. Always learn from the experts because the experts have their knowledge in order. You know what? If your knowledge is not in order, then the more of it you have, the more confused you become. She was not afraid of change in her own life and she made sure that I was not afraid of change. She'd say all meaningful change comes from within. If you really want to change your circumstances on the outside, you've got to make the right choices on the inside.

It is true, every improvement in your life or my life has come as a result of change and yet every change does not always endure improvement, but change is a wonderful thing. If you'll look all around you, timid people are scared of change and comfortable people are threatened by change but confident people think of change as opportunity. Maybe that's why immigrants come to America and they change a dramatic part of their lives, their history, their background, their culture, everything that they know and the belief in their heart that they can make something come to be, gives them that confidence. That confidence leads to commitment and commitment leads to extra ordinary performance. It's L. Ron Hubbard that says, "One machine can do the work of 50 ordinary people, but no machine can not do the work of one extra ordinary person." So, if we want to be extra ordinary, we have to have commitment and to have commitment we have to have confidence and to have confidence we have competence, and to have competence we have to have knowledge, skill and experience. And that is what my mother was so focused on. She'd say focus is a very important part of your life. Focus is more important than intelligence. Highly focused people can achieve dramatic things in their lives.

Wright

Tell us about your early education.

Qubein

Like everybody else, I went to school and then I went undergraduate and then graduate school. In terms of formal education as in schooling, I have undergraduate and graduate degrees in business and human relations. But the greatest piece of my education was listening to a woman who, while she did not possess a lot of formal education, had the wisdom of the ages. She really understood that we must not practice what we preach, we must preach what we practice. When you've got to preach what you practice, you practice the right things. The greatest education in terms of critical thinking and the ability to get along with people and the understanding of what life offers, I received in the home, not just only in the school.

Wright

While researching for this interview, I found that diversity in business seems to be your forte. You're chairman of National Public Relations Company, you're chairman of Great Harvest Bread Company, of course as I mentioned with over 200 stores in 38 states and you started a bank. As an entrepreneur, do you find diversity in business keeps your creativity alive?

Qubein

I do believe in intentional congruent. I believe that if you are involved in a number of businesses you achieve a couple of things. First, you not merely diversify but you hatch. If you diversify like people do in the stock market, they diversify their money in different kinds of stocks, financial and large cap, so on and so forth. But when the market went bad, it didn't matter that you diversified, you got beat pretty much across the board. Had people not merely diversified, they would have had money in stocks, money in bonds, money in real estate, money in cash and money in other businesses and so on. I believe that hedging is a wonderful thing. I personally don't want to have my income to be derived from any singular source. My goal is to have no one stream of income come or no one source of income be responsible from more than 25 percent of my income. In other words, I speak, as you know, and I consult to all kinds of corporations across the country on a regular basis, but I wouldn't even want that to be a very large part of what I do so I can hedge my life in such a way that I can manage my risks. But also when you are involved in a number of businesses you can have one business help the other. For example, my speaking business feeds into our advertising public relations company. Our advertising public relations company feeds into our magazine business. All of my businesses feed into Great Harvest in terms of creating new customers, especially online for us across the country and so on. That's the second reason, intentional congruent helps you to hedge and helps you to build stronger businesses because each one helps the other one become better. And thirdly, it seems to me that it keeps a level of creativity and innovation and excitement and passion about what you do. Because every day is fresh and new, exciting and demanding and challenging. I thrive on that. I certainly don't work to live, I live to work. I am not a workaholic by any stretch of the imagination but I have such a passion for what I do that I truly love the art of business. I find it exciting to be able to serve people and create products and services that render value in a measurable way.

Wright

Are you an active participant in most of the businesses that you get involved with or in other words, are you hands on?

Qubein

Each business has a president and the president basically runs the daily affairs of the business, but I am typically the chairman of the business. I am involved in the sense that I am in contact on a daily basis and have board meetings on a monthly basis. I am not involved in the context that I am running the micro details of the business. That would be practically impossible.

Wright

I also like to diversify for many reasons, most of which you already discussed, however, I've had people all down through my life say, "You really ought to focus on one thing, find out what you're best at and keep on doing it and keep on doing it until you get better and better," but I don't seem to be able to do that. What would you tell our readers who have entrepreneurial spirits that just don't envision themselves doing one thing for the rest of their life?

Qubein

There's nothing wrong with doing one thing for the rest of your life. What you've just described is a reasonable thing. Was it J. Paul Getty that said, "Put all your eggs in one basket and watch that basket pretty closely?" You could make the case for diversification, you could make the case for singular focus in business. It just depends upon what turns you on, what tunes you in, what tunes you up. It just depends on what makes you happy. It depends what kind of skills and talents you have and how you bring them to there. I certainly would agree with the notion that sometimes if you're diffused in your focus that might actually come back to haunt you, not help you. In other words it might take you in all kinds of different directions and you might not really be able to achieve anything of great value. I think both angles, diversification vs. singular interest, one could make the case for either one. But the definition of an entrepreneur is one who likes to meet challenges head on, likes to take some calculated risks, likes to build things from scratch, likes to have his or her fingers in a number of things. For me, I find it more exciting to do all that. Also, in my business as a speaker, author and consultant, it certainly brings a lot of measurable experience that I am able to get involved in these different businesses. Then your engagements or your clients say, "I want to hear that guy speak because that guy really is a businessman and he's proven himself in a number of areas." So, divisibility just adds to the credibility of what you do.

Wright

Many times success allows us the option of giving back to the community a portion of our abundance to those who would strive to succeed. Tell us about the Qubein Foundation and what it has meant to young people.

Qubein

I believe in the words of William Barkley, the Scottish theologian, who said, "Always give without remembering, always receive without forgetting." So, for me it's been a very simple thing, that you must give. It was Winston Churchill who said, "You make a living out of what you give you make a life out of what you give." It was John Wesley who said, "Earn what you can, save what you can, but for heaven sakes, give all you can." I find when we give, giving doesn't always mean money, you can give time, energy, effort, creativity, leadership, coaching, etc. But when we do give, we become better people. I know we become better people because we reach beyond ourselves and we look at life as more than a self-centered, self-serving focus. The Qubein Foundation began in 1973 and it's focus is to help young people go to college. We have 47 young people in college as we speak, we have educated well over 500 young people. We have given over 2 million dollars and I've used all the royalties of my books, cassettes, videos over the years to donate to this foundation. It really came out of passion for me because when I went to college it was by the mercy of God and the help of others that I've been able to make anything come to be in my own life. It was from my heart and my soul that I wanted to help others and philanthropically sometimes you do best when you can focus on one or two areas vs. just spread it all over the place. So, that's what we did. It's been very fulfilling and a very exciting thing to do. It's been wonderful to watch how some of these young people have grown and they've done some spectacular things in their own lives.

Wright

Your book, *How To Get Anything You Want,* discusses the theory that winners are made not born. You write that the book shows how to mobilize all our resources to become all that God created us to be. Could you tell us a little bit about the book?

Qubein

The book, *How To Get Anything You Want,* is a culmination of lessons and fundaments I've learned in my own life about the notion that practically anybody can make their life better, practically anybody can make good things happen in their life if they are willing to work hard enough and smart enough to make it happen. That book sets forth an agenda for how an individual can decide what it is they want most out of life, determine the first step that will get them there and then to do something about it. It's an inspirational, motivational book with strategies that individuals can follow to pursue their dreams.

Wright

Several times in your writings you refer to God. Has faith played an important roll in the decisions you've made in your life?

Qubein

Absolutely! We all come from the salt of the earth, we all go back to the salt of the earth. The book of Genesis said, "God breathed in my nostrils and gave me life." I like that poster that says, "Life is God's gift to me, what I do with it is my gift back to Him." It is without Him I am nothing, so I talk about it in all of my talks. Never in a way that offends anyone, just always in a way that expresses my own feelings and where I'm from and how I feel about things. People surprisingly are very, very warm and very responsive. Matters scriptural are always, always better than matters secular. It doesn't matter how a person measures their own spirituality, they just find greatness in talking about your soul and your needs and who you are as a human being.

Wright

Nido, you're such a fascinating man and a role model for those who would seek to fulfill their dreams and goals. Could you tell our readers about your philosophy that teaches people not only what to do and how to do it but how to think? What do you mean, how to think?

Qubein

Well, the truth is I am, therefore I do. The being state must come before the doing state. You do what you do based on who you are. So, the analogy would be that you're an honest person, therefore you do honest things . Not you do honest things therefore you're an honest person. The explanation would be if there's something you've got to work on, you've got to work on yourself. You've got to work on yourself first and foremost because if you work on yourself and you make yourself the best you can be, good things will come your way. Critical thinking is very important, it's the mindset that we have that defines the person that we become. These thoughts have a way of creeping up on our lives unconsciously, subconsciously, when we least expect them and so we must ensure that what enters our brains does not tear us down. We must make sure we hang around people and we learn from people who are intelligent and who represent the kind of philosophy and kind of life we want to be more like. It's incredibly important to learn how to think. There are many ways to think. You can think fat, you can think big, you can think deep. You can look beyond the surface of issues and think more critically, you can think outside the box and you can even throw out the box and start from scratch. So, how we think pretty much dictates what we do.

Wright

Most of the people that I talk to that know you personally say that you not only teach and talk about honest business, you also live it. What do you think of the dishonesty discovered in business in the recent past?

Qubein

I chart that off as the exception not as to the rule. It is my belief that give me 100 people or 100 businesses you're always going to have a degree of that take place; it is human nature. That is just the way it is. We cannot live our life by the exception; we must live our life by the rule. We can't look at the squeaky wheel to determine what life is all about. I would say the most important thing in business is ethics. You have to be predictable. If you're going to be predictable in anything, be predictable in the area that says you are going to be honest. This says people are going to know how you are going to respond. That's why we say always do the right thing, when you do the right thing you feel better, people are going to like you better and they are going to understand where you are coming from. There will be no guesses about your persona or your character. Someone said reputation is what people think you are, character is what God knows you are. At the end of the day when you lay your head on the pillow you still have to live with you, you still have to look at yourself in the mirror. You still have to get up the next morning and go to work with you. You want to make sure that part we call you is consistent with the good feelings that you can live with and that you find mutually acceptable in your psyche and in your emotions. I wouldn't worry too much about the recent chapters with ethics in business because that will always be here, that's always been here. I would choose to look at the greatest majority who are honest and who are ethical and who have excellent accounting methodology and who are not greedy. Greed is not wealth, wealth is a good thing. Greed is wealth gung ho, just living for that and nothing else.

Wright

For someone who came to the United States without knowing the language, you've become a master communicator. Could you tell us about your book titled, *How To Be A Great Communicator In Person, On Paper and At The Podium?*

Qubein

That's been a best selling book as you may know, and also the cassette program on that called, *How to Communicate Like a Pro,* actually sold millions of dollars at retails and then we started publishing that ourselves and it still sells with great activity. I think the reason is that most people want to know how to communicate effectively with others. In this material I teach the difference between communicating and connecting. I say to communicate you just have to speak, listen, observe and write well. But to connect with people you really have to have a definition of understanding about who these people are. You have to ask questions like how must this person feels first before this person will do what I want them to do? How would I establish a trust bond with this person? How do I get this individual to acknowledge that what I'm sharing with them or what I want them to share with me is for mutual benefit? So, to connect with someone is to go beyond the surface. We teach the transformational, which is how to change a person toward even greater positive steps and the transactional, which is the specific skills, the specific methodology of how to speak, listen, observe and write in a diverse world with all kind of people coming together to form teams, businesses and otherwise.

Wright

I know that you are continually helping other people to become better and more successful, that's obvious in everything you write and in all of your cassette programs. I remember I had the opportunity to hear you speak in Atlanta one time and everything you say seems to be some attempt to help other people to be better. Could you tell us about the people in your life that have influenced you and perhaps caused you to become a better person?

Qubein

You know every one of us needs to have people in our lives. We need to have heroes, models and mentors. We need to have heroes that we can look up to and try to emulate. We need to have models that we can hold up as positions of achievement and we need to have mentors who will take us by the hand and guide us down the highways and bi-ways of life. I have been gifted in my life and blessed in my life with many of those people. My mother of course was first great mentor. I have men and women in business and industry whom I have know over the years that have been wonderful teachers for me, not that they ever called me up to teach me but they always responded to me when I called them up so that I could learn. They say when the student is ready, the teacher appears. I've always had open eyes and open ears and an open mind to learn, to adopt and to adapt from others into my own life. I have a great family and they are very important to me in my life. I have a great teams of business associates through my work and different ventures, they are always a source of information, a source of insight and a source of impact. If all

118

you have is information people will use you, if you have knowledge people will need you, if you have wisdom people will respect you. Information tends to answer this question, "What is it?" You say what is it, somebody gives you information. You say what does it mean, that's insight. You say what do I do, that's impact. So, ultimately the most important people in our lives are not the one's that share with us information, because we can access that in lots of different places, but they are the one's who display and model that information in ways that we can see and feel, and consequently do in our own lives.

Wright

Did your mother live long enough to see you as successful as you are now?

Qubein

Actually, my mother is still living, she is 90 years old. She's had a wonderful journey.

Wright

Not only does she get to watch you but she gets to participate. That is wonderful. This has been a great conversation. If I ever want to know how to be successful I think I'll call you up and let you become my mentor.

Qubein

It was my pleasure chatting with you.

Wright

Thank you so much. We have been talking today with Nido Qubein who is chairman of an international consulting firm and the recipient of so many speaking and consulting awards from National Speakers Association to Toastmasters to colleges, who holds the honor, which is the Ellis Island Medal of Honor. Thank you so much for being with us today.

Qubein

Thank you very much.

About The Author

Nido is a keynote speaker, seminar leader, corporate consultant, successful businessman and author of many books and cassette learning systems. He is a high-energy performer who will inform, entertain and inspire your group. He always provides high-content, take-home value through carefully customized presentations designed to meet each client's specific needs.

Nido Qubein
Creative Services, Inc.
PO Box 6008
High Point, North Carolina 27262
Phone: 336.889.3010
Fax: 336.885.3001
Email: info@nidoqubein.com
Website: www.nidoqubein.com

Chapter 10

SUSAN F. FRUIT, ASID

THE INTERVIEW

David E. Wright (Wright)

Today we're talking with Susan F. Fruit, ASID, a licensed interior designer and residential remodeling contractor who has been actively practicing residential interior design for 30 years. She is a graduate of Purdue University with a degree in Interior Design and a strong background in architectural history and landscape design. Susan is the founder and former director of the University of Houston's Interior Design Certification Program and owner of Design Transformations, an interior design seminar company. The author of numerous articles on interior design, architecture and landscape design, she is a frequent contributing writer to *Houston House & Home* magazine and other publications. She will be writing special home design articles for a new national interior design magazine, *Abundant Living*, launching in January 2004. In addition, she has lectured and taught design classes throughout the U.S. and Canada. A professional speaker and recognized authority on interior design, Susan is one of only three interior designers in the country who have attained professional membership in the National Speakers Association. Ms. Fruit, welcome to *Conversations on Success*.

Susan F. Fruit, ASID (Fruit)
Good Morning, David!

Wright
Susan, as I have looked at your design work and read your articles, I've noticed that there is a common link connecting the many facets of your business. That link seems to be your passion for creating beautiful, tasteful, and timeless interior design. Why is that so important to you?

Fruit
More and more people today long for the comfort, convenience and security that a well designed home provides. They want their homes to be beautiful and tasteful as well as have longevity in terms of style and design. In my residential interior design work and in my design seminars, my mission and passion is to integrate the timeless principles and elements of design, which have been the building blocks of all great design for more than 2,000 years, with interior design tastes, styles, and trends of today. My disciplined, historically referenced approach to creating timeless, tasteful design is what sets me apart from other interior designers and is what my company is known for. It is both exhilarating and challenging for me to be rooted and grounded in classic architecture and design theory and then integrate these traditional concepts into twenty-first century living as I design and create. In the interior design world today, there is an exciting resurgence in all things classic and traditional combined with fabulous new fabrics and finishes, captivating colors, and tantalizing textures. The most popular style of residential architecture today is historically referenced with lots of interesting period details combined with good quality construction, conveniences and character. It's an exciting time to be an interior designer.

Wright
Susan, how did you get started in the interior design business?

Fruit
After my graduation from Purdue University, I started working for an architect and a builder in a design/build firm in the St. Louis area. I was responsible for selecting and coordinating all exterior building materials and interior finishes for their construction projects. That was my initial introduction into the building industry. Lit-

tle did I know then that 30 year later I would come full circle, back to enhancing architectural facades as I did in those early years.

Upon moving to Houston, Texas in 1978, I started teaching interior design classes to homeowners through a local university in order to establish a client base. One design class led to another, and soon I developed a three year curriculum of professional level interior design courses for individuals who wanted to become their own interior designer or who desired to enter the full time practice of interior design. This led me to formally establish and become the director of the Interior Design Certificate Program at the University of Houston. It was an intensive certification program consisting of 23 interior design core courses and 100 elective hours of related design courses. It is gratifying to me that graduates of this program have gone on to become well established successful interior designers in the Houston area and beyond.

While teaching many of the curriculum's core courses and directing the program, I started my own interior design business, Susan F. Fruit Interiors and Landscape Design. At that time, my company included a landscape design business with a crew of five men along with my interior design business. After a while, these two compatible but different businesses got to be too much for one person to handle efficiently, so I discontinued my landscaping business in order to concentrate solely on my interior design clients and to create and grow my interior design seminar business.

As the construction industry thrived in Houston, especially the new home building industry, so grew the residential remodeling market. Since I was already teaching homeowners how to update their homes by upgrading their appliances, finish selections, surfacing materials, color schemes, furnishings, etc., I naturally evolved into becoming a residential remodeling contractor specializing in upscale kitchen and bath design along with my regular interior design practice.

Today, in addition to teaching interior design and home remodeling courses, I also write articles on these topics as well as ones on "architectural face-lifts" and landscape design. Increasing the curb appeal of one's home greatly increases its market value, so I always include advise on how to improve the exterior façade and landscape design in my initial interior design consultations with clients.

When I look back over my career, it's interesting to note that so much of what I am doing now all began 30 years ago when I was a young, budding designer selecting finishing materials for a builder and wishing I could be doing something "more important" than working on the facades of homes.

Wright

In reading some of your articles on your website, I noticed that your tag line is America's Design Detective. Why are you called that?

Fruit

After 30 years of working one-on-one with homeowners on a wide variety of renovation and remodeling projects, I have learned how to quickly diagnose design dilemmas and provide sensible, practical solutions that most homeowners would never have thought of on their own. Like a detective on a case, I analyze and scrutinize every detail that goes into a project, and then create special customized features just for that project so that it will have a unique, personalized look when completed. The clients then have a home that is truly the home of their dreams.

My goal during a remodeling project is to have the homeowners be able to sit back and relax, knowing that they can trust the person they have in charge. As their Design Detective, I handle their "case" by keeping their job moving, on time and on target, and providing sensible design solutions as the need arises. By being attentive to their needs and concerns and by being constantly available, I am able to greatly relieve the worry, stress and frustration that usually accompanies a remodeling or redecorating project.

Wright

I have heard that there is a difference between an interior designer and an interior decorator. What is the difference between the two?

Fruit

Before I answer that question, I think it is important to explain how the interior decorating profession came into being. It's really quite fascinating. So, if you will allow me, I would like to give you a brief overview of the history of the interior decorating profession.

Wright

Certainly.

Fruit

The desire to decorate an interior space is not new. The concept of interior decorating dates back to the beginning of recorded history with prehistoric cave drawings. From the beginning of time, man has sought ways to beautify his environment. An artist's skill level, cultural environment, and available natural resources determined the design and artistry of early interior decoration. Over the centuries, craftsmen, painters, sculptors, architects and even upholsterers and shopkeepers advanced the art and culture of interior embellishment. In France, these latter were called *ensembliers*, since they assembled all the necessary furnishings for an interior. Elaborate manor houses of the wealthy became great showplaces filled with exquisite collections of paintings, sculptures, tapestries, books, manuscripts, and fine hand crafted furniture. The end of the nineteenth century through the first quarter of the twentieth century became known as the age of the great collectors.

Enter the dawn of the twentieth century in America. At this particular time in our history, the typical American residential interior was dark, somber, stuffy and cluttered with late Victorian inspired décor; gilt-framed paintings and elaborate tapestries on the walls, heavy velvet draperies at the windows, numerous oriental carpets on the floors along with suites of ornately embellished furniture. In addition, many American homes in this Victorian era often housed elaborate collections of art objects; fans, portraits, mantel clocks, oriental vases and other bric-a-brac assimilated from years of travel abroad.

This era was ripe and ready for the emergence of a new aesthetic discipline, evolved from the need for one professional person, (instead of many) to coordinate and create a more tasteful, decorative style for American home interiors. Thus emerged a new, artistic professional known as the interior decorator.

Wright

That is an interesting evolution. Do you know who was the first interior decorator in this country?

Fruit

Elsie de Wolfe (1865-1950) was the first and is generally considered the greatest of all of the early professional interior decorators. Before her there was no such thing as an interior decorator or a decorating profession. She literally gave birth to this profession. As was the custom throughout Europe, American architects, painters, sculptors, craftsmen, upholsterers and cabinetmakers traditionally provided interior furnishings and advice to the wealthy clientele who could afford their services. Elsie de Wolfe single-handedly changed that practice. She personally selected and purchased all the decorative components and supervised all the installations that comprised the decoration of her clients' homes. She is credited as being the driving force in helping to transform the dark, dreary Victorian interiors of the day into a new prototype of elegance, refinement, sophistication and good taste. She striped away the excesses of the Victorian age and the many overlays of *things* that the mass production of the Industrial Revolution had made possible. She banished heavy draperies and elaborately carved furniture and in their place introduced Neoclassicism to American interiors. She transformed rooms with the light and elegant eighteenth century French furniture styles of Louis XV and Louis XVI. She painted dark woodwork and furniture white or ivory, (her signature colors) uncovered windows to let in natural light, replaced multitudinous collections of paintings and wall bric-a-brac with one large dramatic painting or one large mirror, and often used a single pattern of chintz for walls, window treatments and all major furniture pieces, decorating simplicity unheard of in its time. Thus began the establishment of personal style in decorating.

Wright

So, it's ok for people to dare to go their one own way in personal decorating?

Fruit

Absolutely. That's why I teach design classes, to introduce homeowners to the classic principles and elements of design so that they can discover their own likes and dislikes which will then help them determine their own personal style. But back to our story about Elsie de Wolfe.

Elsie had a mind for business and professional promotion that matched her creative energy and design abilities. She had business cards printed, (unusual for women at that time) announcing that she was available to "supervise the arrangement and decoration of homes," thus launching her career as a professional tastemaker and interior decorator. She also had the business savvy to establish herself in wealthy social circles. In so doing, she also elevated the social status of this new profession, thus laying the foundation for all twentieth century interior decorating that followed.

By the mid 1920s, the interior decorating profession increased rapidly both in numbers of practitioners and in wealthy clientele, and had spread well beyond the personal practice of Elsie de Wolfe. Many society women decorators who were to become the luminaries of the profession for the next forty to fifty years rose to prominence during this time. Many of them decorated with antiques and antiquities from trendy, upscale Parisian antique shops bought on buying trips to Europe. Since many of the celebrated and successful women decorators had begun their practice as fashion conscious society figures who decorated mainly for their friends and husband's business associates, they were often derogatorily referred to as "The Ladies." In many peoples' minds, they had merely turned the social pastime of shopping into an art form for personal profit. Therefore, for several decades, interior decorating was not always taken seriously. It was often merely considered a "hobby" for the rich and famous.

In contrast to those society ladies who merely dabbled in interior decorating are a number of famous, first-generation professional women decorators who took this new profession and their careers seriously. Along with Elsie de Wolfe are Elsie Cobb Wilson, Nancy McClelland, Ruby Ross Wood, Eleanor McMillen Brown, Rose Cumming, and Francis Elkins, sister of the famous Chicago architect, David Adler. These women and several others are among the most notable and famous of the early professionals. Each of these first generation decorators, as they are known, created their own signature style and introduced their own unique sense of discipline, order, and taste. This in turn earned them an impressive list of clients who eagerly sought out and engaged their decorating services. It is interesting to note that, more than fifty year later, the creative energy, talent, taste, and style that these early decorators became famous for has left an indelible mark on the world of interior design that is still being recognized and studied by design students and professional practitioners today.

The signature design work of these first generation decorators gave rise to the work of the second and third generation of decorators, notably Sibyl Colefax and John Fowler, Mrs. Henry Parrish II (affectionately known as Sister Parrish), Dorothy Draper, Syrie Maugham, wife of prominent author, Somerset Maugham, as well as prominent male decorators such as T. H. Robsjohn-Gibbings, Michael Taylor,

Billy Baldwin, John Dickinson, Albert Hadley, Edward Wormley, and William Pahlmann.

Women's decorating magazines such as House & Garden, House Beautiful, and Vanity Fair among others proliferated on the scene, igniting wide spread interest in interior decorating and succeeded in bringing style and taste within reach of the mainstream middle class. Decorating advice columns in newspapers also helped educate and expose the public to good style and taste.

Over the years, many interior decorating clubs and societies for the professional interior decorator were formed, eventually consolidating in 1975 into one main organization for professional interior designers known as ASID, the American Society of Interior Designers. The last word in the title of the new organization moved away from the previous term "decorator" to the newly designated and elevated term "designer" to reflect the full range and scope of an interior designer's professional responsibilities and design services.

Another important development occurred in the late 1960s through the early 1970s that expanded the boundaries and limitations of the interior decorating field into a broader, more specialized and professionalized arena of design. The interior decorating profession as it first began at the turn of the last century and continuing through its height of popularity throughout the 1950s, was one of selecting, collecting, and arranging decorative items within a room. For those desiring to become an interior decorator, there was very little education available or formal schooling to be had in this "new" profession. During the 1950s and 1960s, a few colleges and universities offered one or two basic courses in interior decorating through their Home Economics or Sociology departments as part of a Home Economics degree. The other route to becoming an interior decorator was to work for a well-established decorating firm or to learn under the tutelage of a famous independent interior decorator.

During the late 1960s however, this began to change. A few select American colleges and universities began to recognize interior design as a viable career option and allowed Fine Arts Departments to develop interior design curriculums with a specific course of study for interior design students. Along with traditional art and design courses, interior design students were now studying space planning, color theory, fabric and textile design, art history, furniture finishes and construction, and so on. During the mid 1970s, architecture and structural design courses were added to enable interior design students to understand the structure of the architectural envelope; the enclosing walls, floors and ceilings in order to correctly plan furniture arrangements and other furnishings for an enclosed space. Today, interior design curriculums have advanced to include courses in both residential and commercial space planning, architecture and building systems, creative problem solving, building codes and ADA compliance, CAD drawing, mechanical and electrical systems, business practices and procedures, plus many others. So, in just thirty years, the interior decorating field has evolved and matured into the respected professional career of interior design.

Today, an interior design professional is a person who is qualified by education, experience, and examination to provide a full range of professional design services such as space planning, design research and analysis, schematic development, budget analysis, select and coordinate furnishings, finishes, fabrics, accessories, create color themes and schemes, prepare architectural drawings, renderings and finish schedules, lighting plans and schedules, oversee and coordinate on-site work performed by project sub-contractors, plus many other professional responsibilities.

So, there you have it, a brief but in-depth overview of the emergence of the interior design profession out of the interior decorating avocation, and an explanation of the difference between an interior decorator and an interior designer.

Wright

Wow, you certainly have enlightened me on what it takes to become an interior designer these days. It's requires a lot more knowledge and education than I ever imagined.

Fruit

It certainly does.

Wright

Susan, when I look at different design styles, I'm always torn between bold, new trends and time-honored traditions because as I see them in the design magazines, they are both appealing to me. Is it normal to be that conflicted?

Fruit

Yes, it's normal, and in fact, it's quite typical.

Wright

Good, I'm not abnormal. That's a wonderful thing to hear.

Fruit

David, you wouldn't be normal if you weren't conflicted. By the way, it's a compliment to *you* because it shows that you have moved from being just mildly curious about interior design into the realm of proactive awareness and sensitivity to good design. I'm pleased to hear that you are so design savvy!

New design trends are constantly breaking on the scene that challenge and stretch the boundaries of established design traditions. This is especially true with color schemes and in the furniture, textiles and accessory markets. It is hard enough for most interior designers and retailers to keep up with all the new trends coming and going let alone the unsuspecting public. Design professionals are the tastemakers and style setters, so it is their job to watch the new trends carefully and stay abreast of the times.

There are some interior designers who actually specialize in mixing time-honored, classic furnishings with bold, contemporary design elements to create an exciting mix. The key to making this work successfully is in anticipating with some degree of accuracy which new trends will have longevity versus those that will have brevity. Sometimes some new trends are so "classy" and maintain such popularity and longevity that they actually become classic design elements in their own right. However, if a designer uses too many mundane "trendy touches" throughout a home, they soon become dated and then the entire design scheme becomes mediocre.

Sometimes, using some fashion fabrics or vibrant colors amidst traditional furnishings can be fun and easy, and can keep a home from looking like a museum. So, don't be afraid to mix the old with the new. That way, you will have your feet in both worlds—you'll be honoring the past while designing forward with the current trends of today.

Wright

At the expense of sounding like a complete novice, would you please explain to me why most designers say that every room needs to have a focal point?

Fruit

Yes, I'd be glad to. Every major room needs a point of origin, a place to which the eye is immediately and repeatedly drawn. It is also a point of reference for all the design elements in the room and therefore should be strong and commanding. A focal point brings interest and drama to a room and sets the stage for the room's overall design scheme. A room's furnishings, fabrics, colors and accessories are greatly influenced by the quality and character of this dominating feature. Therefore, it is imperative for every major room to have a commanding focal point. Without one, a room is weak and ineffective.

There are two main categories of focal points; emphatic and dominant. Emphatic focal points are architectural or structural elements, such as a fireplace, a built-in bookcase, a dramatic window or window treatment. Dominant focal points are non-architectural. They have arranged components comprising their whole, such a furniture grouping or a large picture arrangement.

Good space planning dictates that all major rooms with a focal point are laid out according to a 2/3 - 1/3 division of space. The emphatic focal point is almost always in the 2/3. area with the dominant furniture arrangement coordinated around it. The remaining 1/3 area contains subordinating elements.

One of the most important tasks an interior designer performs is to analyze a room and determine if the main focal point is going to be emphatic or dominant, create the 2/3 - 1/3 division of space with furniture and accessories, and then coordinate these divisions back to the main point of reference, the focal point.

Wright

In your opinion, in interior decorating, what is the number one problem that perplexes homeowners the most?

Fruit

That's an easy question to answer. It is most definitely accessorizing! The reason most people have a hard time accessorizing their homes and integral spaces within their rooms is because they aren't aware that there are three easy steps to creating any accessory arrangement. It's as simple as 1-2-3!

Wright

What are these three easy steps, and will I be able to accessorize like a pro if I know?

Fruit

Hey, that rhymes. And, yes, you will! It's really very simple and fun to do. You just need to know three things:

1.) *how to begin* an accessory arrangement, 2.) the *secret formula* that is the key to creating all beautiful and successful accessory treatments, and 3.) *what kind of accessories* to select and group together to create instant decorating success.

First, *how to begin*. Let's say you have an end table in your Living room that needs accessorizing. Clear off all the objects on the table so you can clearly see the shape and style of the table and not be influenced by any existing accessories. Next, choose an appropriate lamp for the table if you don't already have one that is suitable. Let's say the table is made of wood and has basically straight legs. Select a lamp with a base whose shape and material will contrast harmoniously with your wood table, like a base made of scrolled iron. The lamp base adds decorative contrast to the structural form of the plain table. To add further interest and to make the table appear more important, add a 1/2" thick piece of clear glass custom cut to fit on top of the table. Now you have the foundation and the required vertical element (the lamp) for you to begin your new tabletop arrangement.

The second step is the *secret formula* used by professional designers when they create attractive and dramatic accessory arrangements. This "secret weapon" is called *gradation*. In all well designed accessory arrangements, there should always be *three levels of gradation*. To accomplish this, you need to select interesting accessory objects of various heights, shapes, colors, and textures that you can group together attractively next to your table lamp that will create three distinct "stair steps," or levels of gradation when grouped together.

In the third step you *arrange your grouping*. Place your tallest accessories, let's say they are a collection of 4-5 leather bound books, shoulder to shoulder up close to the lamp base. The straight lines of the books will contrast harmoniously with the scrolled lines of the iron lamp. This stand of books should be approximately 2/3 the height of the lamp base for good scale and proportion. Next to them, you need to add a free form object, such as an oval or round container. A colorful oriental lacquered bowl containing an arrangement of green ivy could be the next level of gradation and provide good contrasting form next to the leather books. The third level of gradation could be a cluster of 3 antique glass inkwells (to tie in with the collection of leather books), or a cluster of 3 small antique wood boxes, or perhaps just one object, such as a porcelain bird nestled beneath the ivy foliage.

You now have *three distinct levels of gradation* in your accessory arrangement. The entire setting, including the table, lamp and the accessories will main attractive and interesting over a long period of time because it adheres to the principles and elements of good design.

Wright

Can you give us some examples of the kinds of accessories that you would recommend for people to buy and collect? They seem to be important elements in a room.

Fruit

They are indeed! In fact, accessories can make or break the look of an entire room. When looking for accessories to complete a room, always remember that antique books, especially antique leather bound books in French, German, or Swedish, accrue in value and add an aura of intelligence and sophistication to your room and arrangements. They also add instant culture and history and look wonderful no matter where you place them or group them.

Other types of books that are nice to collect and good to work with are "coffee table" books. These are typically large scale single subject books with colorful cover jackets on topics most people enjoy, such as travel, history, gardening, art, culture, etc. Large and small decorative wooden boxes, either European or Oriental, also add interest and sophistication to accessory groupings and are wonderful collectables. Other types of wooden boxes that are attractive and easy to group are antique tea caddies. They typically have several species of wood inlaid in interesting patterns on their lids.

Be sure to also collect a few interesting glass and crystal objects for your groupings. They are important because they help to balance out opaque items in accessory arrangements. And, don't forget small collectables, such as antique paperweights, inkwells, magnifying glasses. They are wonderful for third level gradation.

Lastly, prized porcelain and imari pieces are fascinating and colorful. You could display a collection of china or porcelain plates on wall brackets in an interesting pattern, or add symmetrical balance to an arrangement with two large scale matching Chinese urns.

These are just a few examples of a professional designer's main staples in finishing a room's décor. They create instant history, add a timeless look to a room, and can be easily mixed with other accessory pieces.

Wright

In your workshops and design seminars, you teach how to create a *distinctive style*. What is that?

Fruit

A distinctive style is one that is memorable. It is one that uniquely reflects the tastes, interests, desires, and preferences of its owners. That's a tall order to fill, and that's why it's hard for most homeowners to design and decorate their own homes. Style conscious homeowners want a distinctive look for their interiors, but don't always know what distinctive style is let alone how to create it.

In my design classes, I explain the essence of style and its three distinct categories. It's a fascinating study. Time does not permit me to go into detail here about how each style directive is created, but in a nutshell, the three categories of distinctive style are:

1.) **Referred,** which describes sophisticated, classy interiors designed with attention to historic style references, such as Country French, Italianate, Mediterranean, etc.,

2.) **Transferred**, which describes transitional interiors infused with current design trends and fashions and,

3.) **Inferred**, the most complicated of the three to create, which is introspective and reflective of a combination of several design elements.

People are not born with that elusive quality known as "good taste." It is an acquired sensibility that develops over years of time through education, experience and enlightenment. A highly refined sense of style is the ultimate in good taste. That's what is called **distinctive style**.

Wright

Can you tell us what is involved in developing a Master Plan as it relates to remodeling or custom designing one's home?

Fruit

Certainly. There are two different Master Plan strategies that can be helpful to homeowners, whether they're planning a remodeling project, building a new home, redecorating or refurbishing their present home.

Master Plan #1. Let's say you are considering a kitchen and bath remodel of your present home. After determining the total funds available for your project, commit in writing the maximum amount you are willing to spend on the entire project. Let's say it's $25,000.00. Draw up a line item list of all the products you will need or want to purchase for this project. Then do some shopping and research to familiarize yourself with what these items actually cost. With this plan, you will be acting as your own kitchen and bath designer. If you have never remodeled a kitchen or bath before, prepare yourself because you will be in for some sticker shock. I recommend selecting and pricing out items you really love as well as selecting and pricing items you may have to "settle for" if the money runs out. After you have created the design for your remodeling project and priced out all the products and materials that will go into the project, set up an appointment with a remodeling contractor and discuss with him or her your remodeling goals and objectives along with your design concepts and list of products and materials to be installed. Your contractor will get back to you with a price to remodel and supervise your project.

If the total price for all the products, finishing materials, labor, and installation services comes in over your budget allowance, (and it almost always does) then you will have to rethink your design and reselect many or most of your long-dreamed-of-having items and settle instead for those items that will "fit" into your allotted budget. Scaling back on product brands and finishing materials usually causes the overall design concept to be lost or "watered down" also. But, this is what has to be done in order to fit everything into a firmly-committed-to set budget. I don't much care for this kind of plan because I have seen what the end result is of this kind of planning too many times over the years. People usually end up with a less attractive remodel installed with products that were their second, or third, choice. Custom details get cut and quality is severely compromised. However, the one advantage to this plan is that by sticking firmly to a set budget allowance, making everything fit within it, you will finish your remodeling project within budget.

Master Plan #2. A different approach to the remodeling project above would be to engage the services of a good kitchen and bath designer or a licensed interior designer to help you create the kitchen and bath of your dreams. The designer will usually charge you an hourly fee to create the design portion of this project. He or she will reorganize and/or redesign your kitchen and bath and help you select all the appropriate products and finishing materials that will create the style of kitchen and bath you desire. In order to give you a realistic view of what your remodeling project will cost, as part of his or her design fee, your designer will also provide a floor plan with elevations showing the placement of new cabinets, countertops and appliances, and obtain cost estimates from vendors and sub-contractors. Additional design work such a creating a custom backsplash, preparing a reflected ceiling plan with a lighting schedule, selecting colors, finishes, fabrics and furniture for these areas, etc. can also be included in the designer's work.

The price of a designer's design fee to generate a custom designed Master Plan for your remodeling project from concept to completion with all product selections, finishing materials, drawings, sketches and realistic budget projections is well worth the investment in the design service. Once the designer's design proposal is completed and approved by the you, it goes to the remodeling contractor for labor and installation quotes if the designer has not already included those costs in the design proposal. Once the entire proposal with all design concepts and all project costs has been compiled and completed, you will have an accurate picture of how much the entire remodeling project will cost. The plan is not based on cost or time frame but on quality and design concepts.

Obviously, master plan #2 will cost more than master plan #1, but the advantage of the second plan is that it can, if desired, be implemented over a period of time, so that design concepts, client desires, quality products and construction are not cut or compromised. Your design professional will specify which portions of the work need to be done first, second, third, etc. so that your remodeling project will be done in an orderly, expedient manner as funds are available.

So, to recap, one way to remodel or redecorate is to limit design concepts and purchases in order to stay firmly within an established time frame and budget. The other way is to design and furnish your house according to your dreams and be willing to implement your plans over a longer period of time.

Wright

Although I do like to stay within a set budget, it sounds like you get more quality and more of what you really want doing a remodeling project the second way you describe.

Fruit

Yes, you certainly do. The second approach does cost more because you don't skimp on quality to save time or money. That doesn't mean, however, that you have to select the most expensive products that are out there. But it does mean that you or your design professional need to take a lot of time designing and creating up front so that you will get the end product that you really want, because you will undoubtedly have to live with the results of what you have created for a long time. So, my advice is to do lots of design planning up front,(either by yourself or with a professional) and then implement portions of the project over time if money is an issue. In the final analysis, you will love the results of your remodeling and/or redecorating work so much that you will have no regrets.

Wright

I've read that in your design classes you also teach people how to expand their homes without increasing square footage. Can you give us some examples of this?

Fruit

Visually, the way to increase the size of a room without actually adding additional square footage, is to "bump out" a window, meaning, make it into a bay window unit. It will not only open up the room more visually, but also allow for additional seating and storage. Bay window units are wonderful additions in Family rooms and kitchens. Replacing small windows with larger window units dramatically helps enlarge the size of a room by letting in more light, air and exterior views. Be sure to select windows with few or no mullions so that exterior views can be well seen. Atrium and French doors will also enlarge the appearance of a room. So, changing out windows and doors will greatly help enlarge enclosed space and appear to make the room feel much more spacious. Additionally, adding a wood deck with an interesting pergola off any room will also giving you added living space without adding additional enclosed square footage.

Placing a furniture arrangement on the diagonal within a room will also help the room appear more spacious. Nothing increases the sense of space more than a long diagonal line. Furniture arrangements look more dramatic and interesting when placed on diagonal, whether in a large room or a small one. Twin or full size beds can also be placed on diagonal, coming out from a corner. Doing so frees up valuable wall space on both sides of the bed. This is an excellent design solution for small bedrooms.

And speaking of corners, use the corners of your rooms wisely. Don't clutter or obscure them with large plants or use them to store items you don't know what to do with. Instead, why not create a cozy corner with a comfortable, overstuffed chair and ottoman for reading and relaxing, placed on diagonal in the corner, of course. Or, perhaps you could place a small game table on diagonal in a corner that could double as writing desk or bill paying center.

For additional storage space and to increase a sense of depth in a room, think built-ins. Built-in bookcases are warm and inviting and create nice depth in a room. Encase a large window with built-in bookshelves all around and see what wonderful depth is created. You will give your room a whole new perspective and added depth.

Another way to expand your space is to create wall niches in unexpected places, such as in hallways, on stairs, in a powder room or in the foyer. It doesn't have to be a very wide niche to have an effect. Oftentimes just the distance between the wall studs will do nicely. If you would like to create a larger niche, you can usually remove an entire wall stud without any consequence.

To further increase a sense of spaciousness in a room, try using the same fabric on all main furniture pieces as well as for the draperies in your living room, family room or bedroom. If your room is furnished in several styles of traditional décor, this "design trick" will help your furniture pieces look more unified and harmonious. If your furnishings are contemporary, then upholstering them all in the same solid fabric will make the room look sharp and sophisticated. These are just a few design tips and tricks to help our homes look larger and be more spacious.

Wright

The purpose of this book, *Conversations on Success,* is to inspire and encourage our readers to lead more fulfilling lives by the examples of our guest authors and speakers. Susan, is there anyone in your life who has inspired you and enabled you to be the kind of person you are today?

Fruit

Definitely! I can say unequivocally that that person is my mother. She was the guiding light for me throughout my life, encouraging, inspiring, and supporting me in all my endeavors. She instilled in me when I was a young child the love and appreciation for fine art, classical music, gardening and architecture. Wherever we went, she pointed out the beauty around us.

Even though my mother had very little financial resources to work with, she always managed to make things beautiful. From her, I learned how to do a lot with very little. She taught me to find beauty and joy in the simple things, starting with nature and gardening. She would create delight with a homemade seasonal wreath on the front door or surprise with a fragrant bouquet of fresh flowers cut from our garden for our kitchen table. I learned early on how fun and easy it is to group different sizes and shapes of accessories together to create an interesting accessory arrangement and how welcoming to play soft music in the background to create a warm, inviting atmosphere.

Wherever my mother lived, she was constantly beautifying and improving her surroundings, inspiring others by her example. From her tireless decorating efforts and tutelage, I learned the meaning of elegance, taste and style, and developed the desire to share this knowledge with others. This is why I love to teach and give seminars on interior design today.

Without the love, nurturing, support, and encouragement of my mother during my growing up years, I wouldn't be an interior designer today. I owe my love of interior design and the success I have achieved in my life and in my career to her.

Wright

So, your mother was indeed a mentor?

Fruit

Absolutely!

Wright

What do you think makes a great mentor? Do you think that there are certain unique characteristics that all great mentors have in common?

Fruit

Yes, I do. First and foremost, one of the most commendable traits that all great mentors have in common is a strong desire to share their knowledge, to pass on to a protégé valuable information that they have learned through years of hard work. It is part of a natural transition in life, the desire to pass the baton on to the next generation.

Following this desire is the mentor's dream to see his or her protégé achieve and succeed. A mentee's success helps validate the success of the mentor, since the mentor was involved in the tutelage of the protégé. In the process of encouraging and empowering one's protégé, the mentor becomes more empowered. It's a wonderful win-win situation.

Lastly, mentors who have achieved great success in their professional careers have a deep desire to leave a lasting legacy so that what they have accomplished and achieved doesn't die with them. Leaving a lasting legacy involves more than just passing on or transferring information to another person. A legacy is an accomplished, triumphant mission achieved through extraordinary vision and wisdom that leaves a lasting mark on future generations.

The mentoring process has been around for more than 2000 years. It evolved through the centuries as the only way to pass on valuable information to the next generation because no formal education system existed, such as schools or universities. During the Renaissance, mentoring was widely practiced in the artistic and scientific communities. That is one of the reasons why there were such extraordinary advances in those fields during that period of time.

Great mentors are out there in all fields of endeavor. There is an old saying, "when the student is ready, the teacher appears." I encourage people of all ages who wish to *learn more, do more,* and *be more* to find a mentor who is right for them. Becoming involved in a mentoring relationship can change one's life and help one accomplish more than he or she ever dreamed possible.

Wright

Susan, thank you for a very interesting conversation. I really appreciate your insight and in-depth information on design issues that I was not familiar with before. You've certainly taken us deep into the world of interior design. I'm sure our readers have learned a great deal from you today.

Fruit

I hope so.

Wright

We have been talking with Susan F. Fruit, ASID, interior designer and remodeling contractor. It is indeed obvious, Susan, that your energy, enthusiasm, and creative talents are the keys to your success and popularity. Thank you so much for being with us today.

Fruit

Thank you for having me, David. It's been my pleasure.

About The Author

Susan F. Fruit, ASID, a licensed interior designer and residential remodeling contractor who has been actively practicing residential interior design for 30 years. She is a graduate of Purdue University with a degree in Interior Design and a strong background in architectural history and landscape design. Susan is the founder and former director of the University of Houston's Interior Design Certificate Program and owner of Design Transformations, an interior design seminar company. The author of numerous articles on interior design, architecture and landscape design, she is a frequent contributing writer to *Houston House & Home* magazine and other publications. She will be writing special home design articles for a new national interior design magazine, *Abundant Living*, launching in January 2004. In addition, she has lectured and taught design classes throughout the U.S. and Canada. A professional speaker and recognized authority on interior design, Susan is one of only three interior designers in the country who have attained professional membership in NSA, the National Speakers Association.

Susan F. Fruit, ASID

America's Design Detective

14827 Elmont Drive

Houston, Texas 77095

Phone: 281.463.2972

Email: designdetective@houston.rr.com

Website: www.SusanFruitInteriors.com

Chapter 11

WALLY ADAMCHIK

THE INTERVIEW

David E. Wright (Wright)

Today we are talking to Wally Adamchik. In his youth, Wally worked with his father and older brother in the construction business. They taught him the importance of producing top quality work. He learned more about excellence from his mom, the first woman to referee a basketball game in Madison Square Garden. In his senior year at college, Wally served as the school's mascot. As the leprechaun, you did serve as a leprechaun, huh?

Wally Adamchik (Adamchik)

I absolutely did.

Wright

Isn't that wild! As the leprechaun for the Fighting Irish of the University of Notre Dame, he poured 100% of himself into every game every week, laying the foundation of complete commitment that defines his work today. As an officer of Marines, he honed his motivational and leadership skills in training, peacekeeping, and combat operations around the world. Next, he was recognized for award-winning leadership and superior performance at two national restau-

143

rant companies. While a regional manager he earned his Masters of Business Administration at the University of North Carolina at Chapel Hill. He then moved into consulting and speaking. His solutions to clients' needs are practical, profitable, and powerful. Mr. Adamchik, welcome to *Conversations on Success.*

Adamchik

Thank you, David.

Wright

How do you define and measure success, Wally?

Adamchik

The first thing about success is that only I can measure it for *me.* Only I can define it for me, and only you can truly, honestly, measure it and define it for you. For me, success is the accomplishment of a worthy objective. We all are given the same basic hardware when we're born, but we don't necessarily use it to the best of our ability. So, if we're moving consciously toward a defined purpose and vision that we chose for ourselves, then I'd say we're a success. This is what I call the 'who wrote your software' problem, all too often people are living the expectations that someone else put upon them and they are unable to break out of that rut. I see it all the time when I'm coaching. Affluent, well off, seemingly happy people, but they are not fulfilled. They're not doing what they want to be doing. They're not *really* happy, and I would say that they are not a success.

Wright

So, rather than consulting, you actually do more coaching?

Adamchik

It's a component of the business. We speak, we consult, and we do coaching.

Wright

I see.

Adamchik

Coaching is a personal relationship with a business objective. If someone and I are a fit, then a coaching relationship may be appropriate. But ultimately, that successful person is the one who has some element of balance, can look at themselves in the mirror and be comfortable with who they are with an eye on the future they want.

Wright

I remember many years ago down in Waco, Texas, we had a working definition of success, and that was, 'Success is a progressive realization of your own personal, worthwhile, predetermined goals'.

Adamchik

There you go.

Wright

And if any of those words didn't match, we weren't successful. However, they did kind of leave out happiness. What do you think? I mean, should you not be happy if you're truly successful?

Adamchik

Absolutely, and the word I used was "fulfilled." Just the other day I heard Zig Ziglar say, "Happiness is dependent on happenings." Yes happy, but more, a deeper joy or fulfillment on an inner level. David, you said predetermined goals. Who determined those goals and based on what criteria? My definition of success says I choose the goals based on criteria that I choose, not on society saying that I need to be rich, or Mom saying I need to be a doctor. But yes, if you are not happy, if you are not fulfilled, then there is no way by any definition that you're a success.

Wright

So, what does it take to succeed?

Adamchik

Well, again, it comes back to that clear sense of where you're going and where you want to be (which are goals) but also, *a clear sense of self.* That will take some brutal honesty for an objective, candid assessment of where one is and what he or she needs to work on to get to where they want to go. To that predetermined location out there. It's about making right choices. Imagine you're looking at a blank canvas and we're all the way down at the bottom, in the dead center of the thing. That's where we are at any given starting point. Ultimately, I want to get high and to the right, because the very top right corner is success. When I draw this for people, I put a" smiley face" up in that spot. When I die that's where I want to be. At the top and to the left is the ultimate "frown face" and that 'nobody knows the misery I've seen' destiny. In the upper middle at the top of the page, if you just waffle your way through life, is the zone of mediocrity. But I believe we need to make the right choices, and right choices essentially become right turns. As time passes, I move up the canvas, I'm moving to the right as well. Every day I'm presented with choices. Do I cut somebody off in traffic? Do I spend a couple of extra hours at work? Or do I go home and spend time with my family? Do I do that extra half-mile on the treadmill, or do I not even get on the treadmill? All choices I am faced with. And making right choices moves me to the right and moves me towards that predetermined goal or vision out there. That is my ultimate definition of success. Now, I can make left turns also: these are bad choices and mistakes. It's the sum total of all these turns that gets me to my final spot somewhere at the top of the canvas. So, what does it take to succeed? A clear definition of where I want to go and then a very intentional understanding of the decisions I'm making every day along the way to reaching those goals. Essentially what we are talking about here is **personal leadership**.

Wright

Someone had told me many years ago that you don't learn anything from success. Success only builds confidence. You learn from failure. So, when you take these left turns, are you not learning?

Adamchik

Absolutely! It's essential to have a clear sense of self, so after I make a left turn, or a right turn, I know what happened along the way and am able to learn from it. All too often, people repeat the same mistakes—either by default or by some character flaw. But it's that brutal honesty that says, "I know I'm not good at that, so I'm going to stay away from that" or "I'm not good at that and I'm going to get better at that" or "I put myself in that situation and I did well. I'm going to put myself in more of those situations."

Wright

Tell me something new about leadership.

Adamchik

Well, I'm not sure there *is* anything new. There's a book called *The Leadership Bible* which points out the leadership lessons in Scripture, so I guess it's all been said or written a few thousand years ago. There is a lot of great academic research out there these days and there really is a more refined view of leadership today. But when people talk about leadership, or when I talk to people about leadership, they always think in terms of someone else. I ask people to list leaders: Patton, Churchill, FDR, Margaret Thatcher, and Jesus Christ, etc.—these usual names are always mentioned. My question to people is *why not you*? Why not *you* on that list? And they say "Well, that's not me. I'm just not like that." So, the new thing about leadership is—it is not about someone else. It's about you. It's about me. We are all leaders, and we can all become better leaders in our lives, in our organizations, in our families, in our business. So, what is new is that it's not about someone else. It's the personal application of the principle that we can all be leaders. Often people confuse the term "leadership" and "management." These are very different concepts. People will say, "Well, I'm a manager" or, "I'm in a leadership position." Now, very clearly, leaders set direction, they align people and they motivate people. Manager's plan and budget, they organize, and they control. This is the 'tastes great, less filling' concept that I talk about. You remember in the "old days" when Lite Beer from Miller came out, there was no such thing as a diet beer?

Wright

Right.

Adamchik

There was no way you could have a beer that actually tasted good and didn't fill you up. Mutually exclusive concepts, but the advertisers put it together. Well, leadership is about *change* for better results. Management is about *consistency* for better results. Seemingly mutually exclusive but, in fact, intimately related. You can't have one without the other. There needs to be a balance between leadership and management. Our society tends to go to one extreme or the other. So, I would say leadership is not new, but it needs to be applied in the right measure, which brings me to the concept of GUTSS. GUTSS is my brand of leadership.

Wright

Tell me more about GUTSS

Adamchik

It's an acronym. It's not about that 'intestinal fortitude' kind of leadership or courage, although that certainly doesn't hurt. But what I mean is Grace, Urgency, Tenacity, Support, and Scorekeeping. And by Grace, I mean being a good person—a person of character with respect for myself and for others. Notice I said "respect," I didn't say "like." Leadership is not a popularity contest. Far too many people confuse being *liked* with being *respected*. I saw that often in the Marines. Young officers would come in and try to be buddies with their people, mistakenly thinking that if their people liked them, they would follow them. Instead those units were unproductive and these young officers were off to a bad start. Urgency is about getting the job done, a bias for action, the understanding that a fair or decent decision executed in a timely manner is far better than an excellent decision that's never implemented or that's implemented poorly. This sense of urgency is important also, because we truly live in a 24/7 world. As leaders we really do need have to have a bias for action. The "T" is for tenacity. Again, leadership is not a popularity contest, so people are going to challenge you; they are not always going to follow. Leaders need to be able to stick to their guns in pursuit of their ultimate objective. They must demonstrate confidence and courage in the face of people who disagree and don't want to get on board with the initiative. The "S" is for scorekeeping. I authored an article, "Management by Cliché" and one of the clichés I included is "What gets measured gets done." When we are talking about business or personal change, if we measure it, we've got a much better chance of accomplishing the objective. Let's look at losing weight, for example. If I want to lose weight, I've got a better chance of success if I get on the scale every week and count calories every day, as opposed to just getting on the scale 30 days from now and keeping my fingers crossed. Measurement is absolutely important so that we can communicate the metrics to the organization. People can then see them written down, so it's objective. It's not the leader's opinion of how well the group is doing. It's a very clear metric that folks have agreed on. And then finally, the last "S" in GUTSS is about support. Leaders need the support of people around them. Leadership can be lonely, so it is important to be able to reach out to confidantes or a "personal board of directors" perhaps. People who can motivate the motivator.

Wright

So, how do you help people succeed?

Adamchik

Well, one of my favorite definitions of leadership is that a leader creates and sustains in others the belief that they can do something until they can sustain the belief for themselves. So, for a lot of folks, it goes back to what I said earlier: "Why not you as a leader?" I like planting a seed that may not have been there before, tending it, and nurturing it until they can do it for themselves, and beyond that, creating and sustaining the belief for themselves. My overall philosophy about making an impact on people is that it has to be personal. These are my four "p's" of personal relations: The first one is "Personal." I can't make an impact on anybody, I can't help anybody else succeed, if they don't believe that I really care about them. My relationships are personal. They're one-on-one. They're eye-to-eye. They are not casual. The second "P" is Purposeful: not inconsistent, again one-on-one. I'm very intentional about my interactions. I have a very clear understanding of what needs to be accomplished and how I can best help my clients achieve their goals.

The third "P" is for Playfulness or light-heartedness. There's that old commercial of the guy kind of moping to work in the morning, mumbling, "it's time to make the doughnuts." Life is too short (or too long) to go through without having fun. But people often work too hard and don't take time to have fun. So, I want my interactions with people to be enjoyable, because then I can make a greater impact on them. They see that I'm having a good time, that I am "successful" by my own definition, and that they can be successful, too. Persistent is the fourth "P." I know that one interaction with somebody may not change them. There are those cases in which I say something to somebody and they "get it." A light comes on and then they are a ball of fire by themselves and they move on. But generally over time, I need to be consistent in my interactions with folks so they know what to expect. They aren't thinking, "Oh my, which Wally is coming to work today."

As a coach, I help people succeed by *asking the next question*. This lets them think to the root cause of problems. I've read in a number of places that when we ask somebody a question, they'll give us a valid answer, but it's not *'the'* answer. Often, we need to ask that third, fourth, or fifth question to truly get down to the root cause. As a Second Lieutenant, I had a young Marine who was coming to work late. He really was a good kid, and I said to him, "Hey, what's the problem? Why are you coming to work late?" He said, "Well, sir, I'm tired." I could have just chewed him out and left it at that. But I said, "Well, why are you tired?" He said, "Well, I'm up late with the baby." Then, I could have said, "Well, get your wife to take care of that and get to work on time." But I said, "Well, why is that? Why are you spending so much time with the baby?" At which point, he told me that his wife had left him the week before. To which I said, "Okay, time to get the Chaplain involved!" If I never ask those other questions I am unable to look beneath the surface and I can't get to the root cause. By the way, that young Marine got things fixed and continues to make a positive impact in the Corps today. So, I help people succeed by helping them truly understand the root cause of some issues, helping them face themselves with brutal honesty.

Finally, as a speaker, how do I help people succeed? How do I make an impact? Passion and compassion. Passion for my subject and compassion for the audience because I know what it feels like to sit there in the audience and I want them to get something out of what I am saying. It's not about me; it is about them—the audience. The reason I'm up there is I have because I have a gift to be able to reach people through speaking and I've got some unique experiences. It's about the audience taking what I share with them and applying it in their lives. I think the folks I talk to can sense that from me.

Wright

So, what makes you different?

Adamchik

Well, we're all different. We are all given our unique "chemistry." We all have different life experiences. I have faced a variety of situations and learned a lot from them. I applied those lessons later and met with success. My experiences? I grew up in a strong family; I had great role models who gave me solid values, core fundamental values that I still call on. My education is another experience that helped shape who I am. I know there are a lot of folks who have never had any formal schooling and are wildly successful. But my education—being a student at Notre Dame, being the mascot at Notre Dame, gave me the chance to motivate people: to make an impact. Being a Marine officer, representing our country, leading young Marines, learning about people, and operating in real world contingencies, presented me with opportunities for personal growth. Another way of saying all this is that I have been tested and passed the tests.

As a business leader, I've run operations and had P&L responsibility. Every month I had to look at the bottom line. So, I know when I work with businesses, my solutions and my words have got to be profitable for them, certainly in the long term but also in the short run. In every interaction, I understand that we've got to link this to profitability and positive impact. Along with my clients holding me accountable is my "personal board of directors." These are eight professionals whom I trust and respect. They make sure I am walking my talk. They keep me on track.

Wright

What challenges are you facing these days?

Adamchik

It's not just me. People share things with me as a speaker and they say, "Oh, you too?" when I talk about my challenges. We hear a lot about low motivation these days, about the declining work ethic in America. As a consumer I find this a challenge. It's a challenge as I interact with people, as I look for good partners and vendors and suppliers for my business. I do think there is a decline of the work ethic. People want faster, easier, simpler, but at what cost? Everybody is stretched thin. We are trying to move at Internet time in a pony express body. I learned an important lesson a few years ago. I received word from Washington that I had been accepted to US Navy Pilot Training in Pensacola, Florida. At first, I felt that "whoo-hoo" kind of excitement. Then I immediately switched gears and began planning— and worrying. "Gotta work hard.....got to get the best grades....got to get first choice of aircraft....." Then I thought, "Wait a second. You're not going to be there for another seven months, Wally. Why don't you just enjoy the fact that you've been accepted to one of the most prestigious schools in the country?" I realized I deserved, even needed to take time for myself, to take care of myself, to take time to pat myself on the back. If I don't do that I risk burn-out, and then become just a survivor, no longer a thriver. I kept that situation in perspective and did graduate number one in my class and I did get my choice of airplanes. I didn't burn out. I remember that lesson still.

People move so quickly these days, trying to accomplish so much, and they are just surviving, just getting by. They are not thriving. They are not happy, not fulfilled. And because they are not happy, it's tough to interact with them.

Another challenge is the change in buying practices. Buyers want things on their terms—they say, "I want it when I want it, how I want it, and at the lowest possible price." The "relationship" part of business is fading away.

Another big challenge for me is work/family balance. I'm stretched thin just like everybody else. I have a wonderful wife and two great kids, and I want to be with them. But I also love what I do professionally. I truly enjoy going out to talk with people. So, maintaining balance is a challenge. I have been given this gift of speaking and the ability to inspire people. I want to use it. But I also want to come home to my family. And finally, there are those chocolate chip cookies. I have a hard time saying no to chocolate chip cookies. So, that's a challenge as well.

The way I cope with all those challenges is by planning. I've got my long-term goals. I've got my mid-range goals, and my short-term goals. I know when to say "yes" and when to say "no." I have learned that when I say "yes," I say "no." That is, when I say "yes" to being with a certain association next Tuesday at 2:00 o'clock, that from 2:00 o'clock until 5:00 o'clock I have said "no" to every other possibility. "No" to playing golf, "no" to attending a seminar, "no" to being home with my wife and family. So, when I say "yes," I think to myself, what am I saying "no" to? That has really helped me with my time allocation which, in turn, has helped with the work/family balance issue.

Wright

What trends do you think will impact the next few years?

Adamchik

This 24/7 society that I mentioned earlier will continue. The customer-centric nature of business will continue. Consumers are increasingly more demanding. The company that can deliver on those demands at a competitive price is going to be well positioned. There is going to be an on-going battle, or tension, between technology—the great enabler—and touch—the people aspect. Technology can be impersonal, and it can detract from quality relationships that fulfill our lives. So, the 'tech versus touch' tension is going to continue, and even increase. Look at how many communication devices people have: e-mail, cell phone, voice mail, etc. But you can't get them on the phone to talk to them! I've facilitated several panel discussions just in the last couple of weeks, and every panel member said *relationships matter*. We must go out of our way to maintain those business relationships.

Another trend is the continued move to a two-tiered market. Whether you are talking retail, or construction, or media, or restaurant, every single industry has the "mega players" and then "the everybody else." The problem with being "everybody else" is that if you are not a "mega player," you either need to become one (which is really hard to do) or you must become a very specialized niche—or micro player. More and more, we are seeing cases of the megas versus the Mom and the Pop. This trend of continuing consolidation at the top ranks presents new challenges for business people and for me as a consumer. One other trend is changing demographics. Baby-boomers are working longer and retiring later. There is a smaller labor pool to replace them. This will be another challenge for business.

Wright

What are your secrets of success?

Adamchik

If I had any secrets, I'd put them in a can and sell them! You see the books all the time. There are the "leadership secrets" of Attila the Hun and everybody else. But here is the secret, and it is no secret—*there are no leadership secrets.* This goes back to 'why not you for leadership?' People sell themselves short. They read the leadership secrets of Rudy Guiliani or someone else like that. And they think, "Those are Rudy's secrets," or "that worked for Attila the Hun." "My situation is different." The person on the street chooses not to relate to the information in those books. So, again, the secret is that there are no secrets. The minute you stop looking for The Secret, you start becoming successful. You begin to embrace timeless principles, the things that work (although they don't always work immediately). When I started applying those principles in conjunction with my personal vision of reaching "high and to the right place," I became a success and very positive things started happening in my life.

Wright

When you consider your "life canvas" as you referred to it, what is waiting for you up at the top and to the right?

Adamchik

It's about the kind of legacy I want to leave. It's a balance across all the metrics that are important to me—family, spirituality, career, financial, social, mental, physical—those are the components of my life that I set goals in. There are some long-term goals that I look at and say, "That is where I want to be." I want do volunteer work. I want to tithe my time and talents. I want to continue to speak. I want to be able to put my kids through college. I want to retire comfortably someday.

I have an over-arching goal. I want to hike the Appalachian Trail, start to finish. It takes six months to do that. That goal drives itself into several other goal areas because I certainly need to be physically in shape to do it. I need to be financially in shape to be able to take six months off. I need to be in shape with my career so that I can take six months off. I need to be in shape with my family so that they'll either join me along the way or make the trek with me. "High and to the right" means I'm moving continually in the direction of those long-term goals that I've set. I'm also setting new ones, continuing to advance, continuing to make a positive impact on people I know and even people I don't know, like ripples in a pond. It means living up to that definition of success—moving toward a worthwhile objective.

Wright

Well, what an interesting conversation. Wally, I really appreciate the time you've taken with me today. I think that you've really got leadership down.

Adamchik

You do me great honor by saying that, David.

Wright

Today, we have been talking to Wally Adamchik who is himself a leader of business people, a teacher, a consultant, and a professional speaker. Wally, I'm going to spend the rest of the afternoon getting the image of this fighting Marine dancing around in a Leprechaun suit out of my mind.

Adamchik

Well, I went from Kelly green to camouflage green.

Wright

I really appreciate the time you've taken with me.

Adamchik

Thank you!

About The Author

Wally Adamchik is a FireStarter—that someone who ignites the "fire in the belly" of your audience—that passion to achieve and succeed. People respond to his message and that means more successful programs and a higher return on investment from Wally. Tested in the Marines and in business, his real world solutions really work. Listeners walk away knowing they can make a difference–and with everything they need to do it.

Wally Adamchik
FireStarter Speaking and Consulting
Phone: 919.673.9499
Email: wally@beafirestarter.com

Chapter 12

JIM ZIEGLER, CSP

THE INTERVIEW

David E. Wright (Wright)

Today we are talking to James Ziegler, a professional keynote speaker and seminar producer, specializing in business networking, sales, and prosperity seminars. Jim helps people in organizations that want to learn how leverage relationships for increased sales and profits. Jim has earned the prestigious CSP (Certified Speaking Professional) designation with the National Speakers Association. This is the highest earned award any speaker can achieve. High energy and high content, he is an accomplished motivational speaker as well as an in demand keynote speaker. His expertise is business. Sales, sales management, database, and Internet marketing makes him one of the most versatile and sought after keynote speakers on the national scene. His book *The Prosperity Equation, The Entrepreneur's Roadmap To Wealth* has received five-star reviews on amazon.com as well as on the news wire. Teaching others how to become rich through starting a business is an integral part of Jim's seminar and speaking business. As a motivational speaker, Jim is in demand frequently performing radio and television interviews worldwide. Jim Ziegler, welcome to *Conversations on Success.*

Jim Ziegler (Ziegler)

Well, thank you very much. I am glad to be here.

Wright

Jim, in a recent article you wrote for Expert Magazine titled "Power Networking," you talk about relationship building. Can you tell our readers what you mean?

Ziegler

In my book *The Prosperity Equation*, I really delved into that. I have a saying that the most powerful people on earth are those people who influence the most other people. There's a lot of depth in that statement. Money, physical wealth—that really isn't influence. The people who have the greatest power on earth are those people that have the best relationships and ability to leverage those relationships with other people for a common good. If you believe the legend, you are connected, within seven generations, to every other human being on earth. In other words you know somebody who knows somebody who knows somebody who knows somebody who knows somebody who knows everybody on earth. You have just got to find those linkages and you have got to have an inventory or who is in your immediate, as Stephen Covey would say...your immediate circle of influence... and then you would be able to leverage those relationships to build a better quality of life, a better business, as well improving the well-being of everyone you touch. It's an extremely positive, high-energy life's philosophy.

Wright

I received a telephone call about an hour ago from this lady who was looking for Dolly Parton, the entertainer, and I used to be a vocal coach at Dollywood. I can't get to Dolly but I know a man who can. So, they were doing some things for the soldiers in Iraq and they wanted her to put something in there with some pictures and things. She got in touch with her in about an hour and a half. So, that proves your point, because I don't know her from Adam.

Ziegler

Well, one of the things I always ask people in my circles of influence is, "Who do you know that can help me?" No matter what you want out of life, now matter what you want to do or achieve, there's somebody in your circle of influence that knows somebody who knows somebody that can help you do that if they just know which direction you are trying to go. In the words of one of the great philosophers of the 20th century, Mr. Ringo Starr, "I get by with a little help from my friends."

Wright

That's right. You know I really enjoyed your book *The Prosperity Equation, The Entrepreneur's Roadmap To Wealth.* To whom did you write the book and why did you write it?

Ziegler

As I am sure you are aware, I dedicated it to my wife, Deborah, and my son, Zachary. The inscription says, "Everything I did, I did it for us." That's so true because when I started my first corporation on the kitchen table back in 1986, my wife was right there with me, shoulder-to-shoulder, and we were stepping way out there into uncharted territory, doing things we had never done before. We didn't even have a business model. Nobody had ever done the type of business I was trying to start—this was a combination of pure innovation and guts—and it was scary. At the time I was a $200,000 a year executive and now here I was jumping out there without a net, starting a new business. My wife thought I was crazy and, actually, looking back, she was right. So, all the chances, all the risks we took, everything we did back in those struggling early years as we were building these corporations, I did it for us. So, I dedicated the book to our family. We all participated. Through the years I have been blessed with celebrity, recognition and applause while my wife and son worked and sacrificed in the background. They deserve to be celebrated by me.

Wright

You have written about the four cornerstone pillars of the prosperity equation. Can you tell us a little, first can you tell us what they are and a little bit about them?

Ziegler

When I was first starting out, formulating a business philosophy, I read the book *Think and Grow Rich* by Napoleon Hill which is a classic, it's a must read. Even though it was written back in the 30s, at the time Napoleon Hill studied all of the wealthiest people of that time and what attributes and characteristics made them successful and wealthy. Model yourself after successful people is one of the cornerstone sub pillars of the equation. I started looking at the successful people I knew. They all had four common characteristics. They had **Attitude**, **Desire**, **Work Ethic**, and **Competency**, the four cornerstone pillars of prosperity according to my book. A lot of people have "Attitude," but unfortunately it's negative. My attitude is focused, intense, and it's right on. I saturate my mind with successful things every moment of my life. I think about success. That's Attitude.

Desire? I've got to tell you most people are secretly satisfied with where they are and what they have. Whether they admit it or not, life is not a lottery ticket. To be successful you've got to have the burning desire to achieve. Of course, "Work Ethic," that should be self-explanatory. Most people are not willing to do what it takes to get what they say they want. So many people out there are stuck with a retirement mentality, that vacation mentality that they put in front of their work ethic. Most people who tell me to stop and smell the roses can't afford any darn roses.

Wright

Right.

Ziegler

That's a fact. So, the Work Ethic is extremely important. If you want it, you've got to be willing to do it. I'm not the wealthiest man in the planet. I don't even profess to be. There are probably people living in every neighborhood who are wealthier than I am. I'm not a billionaire. I don't know how to do that and I've never done that. So if somebody wants to buy my book to be a billionaire, they've bought the wrong book. But I do know how to be at a certain level, which is a pretty good level. I am a low level millionaire if you will. But, in addition to the Work Ethic that brought me here, there are other facets in the equation. The fourth pillar of prosperity, you have to achieve Competency. You've got to be good at something if you expect your business to have value that others will pay for. You've got to have a marketable skill, a marketable product. There has got to be something really competent in your business acumen. Those are the four pillars. If someone is not a millionaire, or at least headed in that direction, I have to ask which piece of the puzzle are you missing?

Wright

As an employer of several people a year, both salaried employees and 1099 people who do things for us, the Work Ethic seems to be the most common missing element in today's society. I question it more and more each year. Do you think there is a reason for that?

Ziegler

Well, I hate to say it. Although there are certainly many exceptions...and I realize you can't pin a blanket generalization on any generation, but basically, in my opinion, "Generation X" is pretty lazy and worthless. I'm sorry. I interview thousands of people in that age category and I don't see the loyalty to the employer; I don't see that most of them have the Work Ethic or some of the other positive qualities I describe in this book. Today's generation seems to be all about themselves and their quality time off. During interviews, the interviewees are asking me about how much time off they get before they ask me how much money they are paid or what the advancement opportunities are. They aren't as concerned about a career path as they are about their vacations.

Wright

Oh, I know.

Ziegler

That whole generation got lost in leisure.

Wright

You also wrote that money is freedom and that most people have difficulty grasping the concept. So what do you mean by money is freedom?

Ziegler

Most people don't have enough money. Now the category of enough money or the concept of enough money—I bought a pretty substantial ring here a couple of years back. It's four and a half carats, extremely expensive, a real eye-catcher, suffice it to say, it's a really nice ring. When I was in the process of purchasing the ring I said, "I'll take it. How much is it?" Most people cannot say those words in that order. They haven't got the freedom to do that. They have to check their finances before they know whether or not they can buy it. Two weeks ago my wife, my son, and I went to Aruba, and we planned that trip with about five days notice. That's freedom, the freedom to make choices in your life, the freedom to be your own employer. In the book I talk about the wealthiest people on earth are not employees. The book is about starting and growing your own business and acquiring wealth. I grew up tough, in a neighborhood where you had scramble to make it, with a high school education and poor parents. Nothing was given to me. Any successes we have, everything we have achieved has been self-made and self-attained. Most people, who are legitimately wealthy, prosperous and successful, paid for it and they deserve what they have.

Wright

And appreciated I might add.

Ziegler

Very much so.

Wright

You know you write very lovingly about your father. Could you tell us about him and how he impacted your life?

Ziegler

I don't know if we have all that much time. I could talk about my dad forever. My dad was a Chief Petty Officer, an enlisted man in the U.S. Navy, 34 years. He was an E-9, the highest enlisted rank. We called him "Chief." Chief fought in three wars, served in the Pacific in World War II and I think he made 17 peacetime cruises. He was aboard the Enterprise during the Blockade of Cuba...Chief was right there up front in the middle of a lot of history. The old man had values. He only had an eighth grade education, but he was probably the most intelligent and well-read man I ever met. He taught me honor. He taught me honesty. Many times I've strayed from dead center, but his values always brought me back. I remember when dad died. The last time I spoke to the old man—he had a cancer—a long drawn out thing—I knew he was never going to get out of that bed. He was crying. Then he became quiet and pensive...Chief looked at me squarely in the eye and said, "Son, I wish I had done all the things I wanted to do." I realized that he had grown up in that depression era and his whole life was involved in playing it safe and not taking any risks. He died with so many things left unfulfilled...things he would have liked to have accomplished. That's one of the parts of the book when I really became emotional as I was writing it. I would hate to know that I stood at the plate and watched three pitches go by and never swung the bat. David, does that make good sense to you?

Wright

It makes absolute sense to me. I hope it makes a lot of sense to our readers. One of the most important elements of the prosperity equation I learned from your book was to leverage other people's experience. I know all there is to know about leveraging other people's money, I think. I used to own a mortgage company. Don't most employers find it difficult to employ people that they perceive to be smarter or more experienced than they?

Ziegler

Well, I don't personally. I can't speak for most employers, but when I hire my people I want people that have a skill, have creativity, and have the ability to grow with minimum supervision. When I teach my employees the vision, what we are trying to accomplish, I want to get out of their way and let them do their best. I grow people to their ultimate potential.

Wright

The sad fact that I've learned through people like Brian Tracey and others that work in recruiting and hiring is that statistically when someone goes in for a job interview, the person doing the interviewing talks about 90 percent of the time and the person who is being hired talks 10. It is very, very difficult with that kind of equation to hire good people. But they tell me, all the books that I read tell me, that that's typical throughout the corporate world.

Ziegler

You know it is. Unfortunately low-level employees hire most new employees. If you want to have a company or an organization that exudes excellence, the highest-level management needs to hire most of the people who are hired because people who are fives hire people who are threes, while tens hire eights. So the idea that if I have an employee working for my corporation or any of the consulting projects that I have, we want top management interviewing these applicants or at least as high a level as we can justify.

Wright

You know I was really surprised that you actually wrote about God in your book about prosperity. Down through the years has faith played a role in your decision making process?

Ziegler

I will say unequivocally I am a Christian. I don't profess to be the ultimate Christian...certainly not someone who would be your role model of the Christian lifestyle. Like I said, I grew up tough and many of my life's lessons were learned on the streets. I've done many things I am not proud of...I am still a work in progress. I would certainly not suggest that anyone would use me as their guide on how to live as a Christian. I have strayed many times, but I always come back to dead center. I'm not writing a book about religion, but it had to be said. There has got to be somebody higher and greater than yourself. I'm not telling the readers or the listeners who your god is. I know who my God is, I speak to Him every day and I am quite comfortable with that. I didn't write to go on a rant. I'm a Methodist, if that's important. When we met, my wife was a Baptist and I was a Lutheran. I wasn't going to be a Baptist and she wasn't going to be a Lutheran, so we just decided we'd be Methodists."

Wright

Now, that's the art of compromise.

Ziegler

Well, Lutherans are sort of staid people, they are sort of stiff and stodgy. On the other hand, those Baptists seemed to sing and have a good time, as long someone doesn't think they're dancing. So...we compromised. So, many people say to me, and this always irks me, its almost as if there is some sacrilegious or unrighteous about being wealthy. It doesn't say that money is the root of all evil; it says the love of money. Jesus of Nazareth was a carpenter.

Wright

Right.

Ziegler

I don't know if you have seen pictures of or visited the Holy Land, but there appears to be a severe shortage of wood. That was the Bill Gates profession of the day. I am certain that Jesus was a businessperson and there's nothing wrong or unrighteous about that in any way. It's the honor and the ethics that you employ that have more to do with it than the accumulation of wealth.

Wright

Most people that have been in business for any length of time at least have had ups and downs, and most of the entrepreneurs have had really, really downs and really, really ups. I was fascinated by you writing, as a matter of fact you wrote in great detail, about being over a half million dollars down in short term debt on December of 1991 and how you overcame it. Could you describe some of those events when your business came to a screeching halt?

Ziegler

It is absolutely astounding that you would mention that at this time. Just last evening I had an experience that brought that back into focus. We are in a process of moving to a new home, and last evening I was shredding some old documents we had in storage left-over from that era. In 1991 when the Gulf War hit, I had consultants on the streets, at times I had as many as 25. These were high-dollar employees; they all had my Corporate American Express card. We were grossing millions, actually more gross revenues than I am making today. When the Gulf War hit business stopped. Stopped is not accurate, it ground to a screeching halt...and...I wasn't prepared to handle it financially. We had started the corporation in 1986 and because it was growing so fast it was extremely fragile. We were pouring all of the money back into the company to drive growth. We were stretched very thin financially. There wasn't a huge cash reserve and now, all of a sudden, in the blink of an eye, I found myself a half million dollars upside down in short-term debt, most of it with the IRS. Now when you talk about that, I had withheld money from these people's payroll and had not submitted it to the U.S. government. Technically that's a crime.

Wright

Right.

Ziegler

I can clearly recall the night I woke up with my heart racing out of control, palpitating in what seemed to be a dead flutter. Here I was just trying to scramble trying to figure out what to do next. My wife and I stayed up most of the rest of that night and when the sun came up we had a battle plan. We contacted everybody we owed money to and worked out a repayment plan that we could live with. Of course the big players we owed the most money to were American Express, Diners Club, and the landlord. Our offices were extravagant, something like 8000 square feet in an upscale building. The one creditor I feared the most was IRS and you know what? They worked with us. The IRS was the most pliable, and cooperative creditor of all. I called the lady at IRS and explained what was happening. I'll tell you, as long as you come clean and say, "Look, this is what's happening to us, we've got a good heart; we're not trying to be dishonorable." We set up a prepayment plan with the IRS and all of the other creditors and now, all we had to do was find some new business.

The first working day of January of 1992, I got on the telephone; Bear in mind I had laid off all the employees; I'm sitting in our office with one employee, an older man who was a dear friend, who said, "Jim, I'll stay without pay." He was handing me the numbers out of the computer and I was making the phone calls. I called every client that we had ever done business with; I was making a hundred phone contacts a day. We were calling across the country, across the time zones, so at 8:00 P.M. eastern time I'm still calling California. I think we raised $160,000 in short-term money, which was a godsend. The half million dollars we were upside down? We repaid it 100 percent plus all of the penalties in less than 14 months. And never...we never ever had any bad credit as a result—not my personal credit; not my business credit. To this day our credit is perfect and we operate 100 percent debt free. I will put as much as $100,000 a month on credit cards and pay it in full every month. We own every stick of furniture and every computer in our offices...more than 6000 square feet of up-scale offices...we're back to extravagant again. During that time we were advised to bankrupt but instead we stuck it out and worked our way through it. That's where the chapter in the book comes through. There is no problem on earth that you can't sell your way out of.

Wright

I was fascinated by the whole story. Most people who find themselves in that position, and I think all business owners at one time at some level does, the first thing you want to do is run from it. You know not make the phone calls. So, making the phone calls I imagine takes a lot of character.

Ziegler

It took a lot of fortitude and we had leveraged the house, we had borrowed to the limit every credit line we had; our back was against the wall. We came out of it. We're doing just over three and a half million dollars today with eleven employees and upscale facilities. Today our life is incredible. Looking back at what happened to us then, if the same situation were to happen we are financially and emotionally prepared to weather any storm. But at that time I wasn't prepared for that eventuality. I was throwing every nickel back into growth.

Wright

Perhaps all those characteristics that you talked about your father paid off in 1991.

Ziegler

Dad was a good, honest, honorable, hard working man but I think it was my mother who taught me salesmanship.

Wright

That's right. You've written that technology has changed all the rules in your business. Could you explain what you are talking about?

Ziegler

Right now I have got 16 up and running websites producing upwards of $60,000 every month.

Wright

That's good.

Ziegler

Our revenues come from diverse multiple streams...seminar sales, product sales, keynote platform speaking, and retail consulting as well as book sales. Technology allows the entrepreneur to compete with giants on a level playing field. It enables me to keep a lot of balls in the air without dropping any. We didn't have the ability to manage this many projects simultaneously in the old days. Just a few years ago the most cutting edge business communications technology was the fax machine. If you can think back to the 70s and the 80s before the cell phone, we were living in the Stone Age. Today we take cell phones for granted. Little kids and senior citizens and people from all walks of life have them. But the freedom of business and motion that cell phones allowed us, you look at that and think about what it has done for our efficiency and how it has increased our productivity...it's awesome.

In my early 20s I was a radio advertising sales person at WAPE Radio in Jacksonville. Here I was driving around all day, making sales calls from business to business in the largest land area city in the world. If I would have had a cell phone then, how much would that have increased my productivity to be able to communicate with clients on my way to clients. The cell phone, and e-mail and the Internet—it is mind-boggling how technology has increased our effectiveness. I'm an expert on small business database applications. In my little operation we have upwards of 40,000 hard names, addresses, and other collative information in my personal database, my business database. We've got almost as many contacts in our e-mail databases. I travel with 40,000 clients contacts and information in my laptop.

Wright

Goodness.

Ziegler

So, the ability to contact people instantaneously at very low cost to advertise, to transact money transactions over the internet by credit card and have the money automatically dropped into your bank account. Who would have thought?

Wright

Right.

Ziegler

I made money last night while I was asleep. I am making more money right now while I am talking to you now. David, this is incredible!

Wright

Right, oh I know. I was pulled kicking and screaming into the 21st century as far as the Internet was concerned.

Ziegler

You're what I call a "techno-phobe."

Wright

I purchased a publishing company and the first day after I bought it I got this e-mail. This company out in Oregon wanted to buy 6,700 books and the books were $20 apiece. I thought they had made a mistake and wanted 6 or 7. So, I called them on the phone and they said, "No, we want 6,700." I had never sold anything except face to face before in my life, and to use the internet like that is just so foreign to me but it didn't take me long to get used to it, I can tell you that.

Ziegler

I guess that cured your techno-phobia? Let me tell you, I am also techno-phobic. I doubt if I can even load some of the programs into my computer. I have a fulltime tech on the payroll who does that for me. But you don't have to know the technology, that's the big misconception. You just have to know what the technology can do.

Wright

Right.

Ziegler

I admit it...I'm techno-phobic. Personally, I'm technologically challenged. But you see, I don't know how to fix a car either, but I can drive one. I can drive the Internet. You don't need to know how to fix it or build it. You don't need to know the technology. All you need to do is know how to drive the applications and what they'll do. Does that make good sense?

Wright

Absolutely. Jim, with our *Conversations on Success* book we are trying to encourage our readers to be better, to live better, and to be more fulfilled by listening to the examples of our guests. Is there anything or anyone in your life that has made a difference for you and helped you to become a better person, perhaps other than your mother and father?

Ziegler

What a tough question! There are so many people, but there was an incredible sales trainer in the automobile industry named Jackie B. Cooper. I wish I had known him better, but we had several wonderful conversations. He was actually the inspiration that caused me to start my own training company. He was an awesome role model. I blew into Atlanta in 1982 with my mattresses tied to the roof of a buy-here, pay-here car. I was broke; I was divorced; I was angry; and within five years I was a millionaire. That story is somewhere in the middle of the book there somewhere. During that time I met Jackie Cooper and somewhere in the middle of that story I became a success. It's all in the book, but I would have to say Jackie B. Cooper was a major influence in my life story.

Wright

That name is so familiar to me. I published a book on selling cars a year ago, and I think his name came up. I don't know, is he a trainer?

Ziegler

Well David, Jackie died...I think it was March 26, 2001, if my memory is correct. He left a legacy to hundreds of thousands of people in the retail automobile industry. I wrote a short obituary for him as a footnote in one of my magazine columns.

Wright

Yes, I remember the author of the selling cars book quoted him several different times. I didn't know him personally, but he must have been a great man.

Ziegler

The thing about Jackie B. Cooper, and there are many, many mentors in my life, but Jackie was a guy that started an industry as an entrepreneur without a corporation behind him. I have built on what he's done and now I am a celebrity speaker in that industry. Most recently I have even had people at conventions asking for my autograph. It's getting to be a lot of fun being me. If you read the book *Think and Grow Rich* by Napoleon Hill, one of the key things Hill talks about is to build a mastermind to leverage the experience of other people because you don't know everything by yourself. Why try to recreate everything. If I was on a dessert island today I couldn't invent a light bulb. I couldn't build one if I knew how to build one, not from raw materials. You have to leverage the experience as well as the productivity of those people that came before you and build on that.

Wright

In your book I remember somewhere along the last part of it where you talk about advertising and marketing and sales which was what I was really interested in. I do a lot of that myself and just collecting names and their e-mails just as a step, if you keep doing that over the years, you talk about telephone touches and just keeping in touch with people and that sort of thing. It's really all about that in itself, a Work Ethic, don't you think?

Ziegler

I would make a hundred phone contacts a day. Not often long drawn out conversations, many times I would just say, "Hey John, Jim Ziegler. Look, I really didn't have an agenda for this call and I don't really need anything. I just want to see how you are doing, how's your business, how is your family?" ...and I database and diary all of my conversations. Every time I speak to somebody, if I pick up a piece of information that will go into my computer database. Next time we speak I might say, "Did your son make the team? How did your daughter's graduation go?" I build up complete profiles on everybody I know.

Wright

That's great. What do you think makes up a great mentor? In other words, are there characteristics that mentors seem to have in common?

Ziegler

First of all mentors have to be where I want to be. You talk about leveraging the experience of other people. I'm looking for those people that have those experiences that I would like to have. Dr. Frederick S. Pearls once said that you are the result of every thing that you have ever experienced in that point to which it has brought you. So, I'm looking for people with experiential credentials. I spoke at a commencement of a college recently in south Florida. For me, a high school graduate, standing up there speaking to professors and college graduates, that was kind of interesting. One of the things I told the graduates...I said, "You know your education is only a credential. Experience is the only true qualification. I know so many frustrated Ph.D.'s that are angry because their education didn't make them successful. It's only a credential; you have got to go do it." People don't want to know what you learned they want to know what you did.

That's the people I seek out for mentors. I actively seek those people out and I actively leverage their experience. Jackie B. Cooper and there's so many people.

The majority of my clients in retail consulting and marketing are still retail automobile dealers; I do a lot of marketing there. Every town I visit I seek out the number one sales person in that market. I'll take them to lunch. I want to know what made you successful. All my credentials were not as much in sales as they were in management and I seek out record setting managers. What makes you successful? You see David, the business philosophy that has made me the most successful as a consultant is simply this...I would want to know what the big dog does.

Wright

Right.

Ziegler

Seek out the big dogs and learn how they became the big dog.

Wright

Well, this has been an exciting conversation. I have not only enjoyed it, I've learned a lot and I really appreciate it. You're not that far away from me, I just may make a mentor out of you.

Ziegler

Welcome, any time. Come on down. If I am in town, my door is always open. I love helping people.

Wright

Today we have been talking to James Ziegler. He is a professional keynote speaker, a seminar producer. He specializes in business networking, sales, and prosperity. His book *The Prosperity Equation, The Entrepreneur's Roadmap To Wealth*...take it from me, Jim's book is really worth the read and the study. It's a great way to understand the principles that you need to know to enjoy life and become wealthy. Jim, thank you so much for being a part of this program today.

Ziegler

Thank you for having me.

About The Author

Jim helps people and companies to realize the explosive dynamics of leveraging relationships for increased sales and profitability. James A. Ziegler, CSP is a been-there, done that, professional speaker with offices in Atlanta. Magazine Columnist, Author and Professional Speaker...Jim is available for Keynote Speeches, Private Business Seminars and Chamber of Commerce Events with expertise in Business Sales, Sales Management, E-Commerce, Marketing and Consulting.

James A. Ziegler, CSP

Ziegler Dynamics, Inc.

3950 Shackleford Road Suite 100

Duluth, Georgia 30096

Phone: 800.726.0510

FAX: 770.921.4440

Email: JamesZiegler@TheProsperityEquation.com

Website: www.ZieglerDynamics.com

Website: www.TheProsperityEquation.com

Website: www.ZieglerSupersystems.com

Chapter 13

JUDI FINNERAN

THE INTERVIEW

David E. Wright (Wright)

Today we're talking to Judi Finneran. Judi has been professionally speaking for over 20 years to groups ranging in size from 5 to 500. Judi's style is dynamic, vibrant and passionate. The most engaging aspect of Judi is her unabashed enthusiasm for whatever topic she is speaking about. She provides useful tools and ideas to allow participants to put their new-found knowledge into practice immediately to create the changes they are looking for in their life. Judi presents topics on many varied subjects, but her passion lies in the area of human potential, life purpose, mission, law of attraction, power of thoughts, synchronicity, intuition, motivation, inspiration, cause and effect, and manifesting your dreams. Judi, welcome to *Conversations on Success*.

Judi Finneran (Finneran)

Thank you, David. I'm excited to be here.

Wright

You were a successful real estate agent making a great income. What made you decide to go into coaching, which meant starting all over again business-wise and financially?

Finneran

Well, I had been coaching real estate agents all over North America for two years on how to improve their business and be successful realtors. At one point I realized if they were happy in their life—if their life was flowing—then their business would automatically flow. I decided I was more interested in working with people on redesigning their life and living the life of their dreams, than their business. I felt drawn to working with people in discovering their untapped potential.

Wright

You and I come from similar backgrounds. When I got my company up to—the largest year I had we closed 1,100 single-family dwellings, that would be 100,000,000 today—and I basically did the same thing. I contacted and hired people like you that would come in and improve their life and I found that it was a lot better than improving their sales skills.

Finneran

That's exactly what I mean and with a broader application than their business life.

Wright

How do you manage all of the competing demands on your time: family, real estate, coaching, and all the other things that you do?

Finneran

I am very fortunate in having a wonderful support team. I have a husband who is 100 percent supportive, my own personal coach I work with weekly and great clients. My favorite quote is "When you are doing what you're meant to do, the universe supports your every step." All of the people in my life are there for a reason.

Wright

What could I expect to learn from you if I became one of your coaching clients?

Finneran

The main message I want to convey to all of my clients is most importantly, they are perfect just the way they are. They have so much unexpressed potential and untapped talent they can use to design and really live the life they truly want. I want them to know and believe there is not anything they cannot do.

Wright

How did you prepare for being a life coach? What kind of ongoing preparation or education do you participate in now?

Finneran

Number one, I am personally coached and have been coached for nine years. The basis of my preparation comes from living my life each day, seeing the changes, which happen as a result of being coached in my own life and the lives of my clients. I've also had training in leadership skills, professional speaking, creating and setting plans etc. My bachelor's degree is in psychology and I am able to put it to good use in coaching. I am always reading, taking classes and constantly working on my own personal growth, all of which I incorporate into my coaching business. I am also extremely fortunate to be one of only 29 Certified Dream Coaches™ in the world, personally trained by Marcia Wieder, America's Dream Coach™.

Wright

What are the most important lessons you've learned from being a coach? In other words, what do you feel is your biggest contribution to others?

Finneran

I am told my biggest contribution to my clients is offering them unconditional support and encouragement. A client recently shared with me her belief I had a gift in making her feel as if she were the most important, if not the only coaching client I have. The lesson I learned from my first coach was to believe in me my clients more than they believe in themselves, which enables each person to develop self-confidence in their ability to follow their dreams. David, I absolutely believe completely in each of my clients or I would not be able to coach them.

Wright

What will your business look like in a year from now or perhaps five years from now?

Finneran

A year from now I intend to be removed from the day-to-day real estate business and be coaching, writing and speaking full time. I will have my first book on "overcoming the fear of our own greatness" published and will be working on my second book about the struggle people have with weight. In five years, I plan to be living in my ocean-front home in Maui, coaching clients worldwide, from my deck. The deck is off my koa wood paneled office, which has a whole wall open to the sounds and beauty of the ocean just below.

Wright

Hmmm. That'd be nice, wouldn't it?

Finneran

I have been refining and fine tuning this dream along with my whole family for several years. I have a picture in my mind of the house, the yard, even the pink crushed abalone shell circular driveway.

Wright

What is your advice to someone who is not clear about what their path is and how to find it?

Finneran

I would say there are two things I would recommend. First, I would suggest they immediately start working with a personal coach, either a professional coach or a dream partner. Someone who will support them and hold them accountable to the time and activities required in making their dreams a reality. Second, to take time out of their busy life, to set aside a minimum of an hour a day for self-discovery, to explore what really interests them by journaling, meditation, reading etc. What are they passionate about? What would they really like to be doing?

Wright

How did you learn to be a powerful speaker?

Finneran

Dave, the power in my speaking is simply a reflection of how passionately I believe in what I am saying. I have been a Weight Watchers group leader off and on over the past 25 years. When I began, I discovered how much I loved sharing those things I believed with groups of people. I'm very passionate about life, and the power is founded on the absolute belief and conviction I have in my topics. I heard a line in a poem today, which said "I want my spirit and soul to dance each day" and that is the message I want to share and encourage my clients to live daily.

Wright

What are you doing in the way of continuing education and how do you find time for this commitment?

Finneran

I'm reading constantly and I usually have about ten books being read at the same time. I'm always looking for people whose styles and techniques I admire and incorporate them. Also, I am always taking a number of classes: currently, a writing class with Suzanne Falter-Barnes, who wrote, *How Much Joy Can You Stand*. I conduct tele-classes with groups of people to understand how others view particular topics. Starting next week, I will be facilitating a ten-week course on Alan Cohen's best-selling new book, "Why Your Life Sucks." I consciously make the time because I know it is important to me a person as well as a coach.

Wright

How do you stay motivated and on track?

Finneran

People frequently ask me "How do you do everything you do?" My answer is it just seems to happen because I am so excited about what I am doing. I'm motivated because I am having fun, doing what I love!

Wright

I understand that you're working on several books. Can you tell us a little bit about what they are about and when they will be available?

Finneran

I'd be delighted to. One of them is about weight. Weight is an issue I've personally struggled with in my life. The book will be about how the weight is symptomatic of how we feel about ourselves. When we learn to accept and love ourselves we can stop worrying about the weight because it'll just disappear on its own. The other one is on our fear of success. That's the one I'm working on now which should be available in six months to a year.

Wright

How did you choose the name? Is it, Dharma Coaching?

Finneran

Dharma Coaching. Dharma is a Sanskrit word meaning "purpose in life." My coaching business is based on my belief each person has a specific, divine reason, role or mission they are in this world for. If their unique purpose is not expressed, no one else can do it for them. I believe my gift, my purpose, my DHARMA is helping people discover, believe in and share their gift with the world.

Wright

You say that your role as a coach is to be a mirror. What does that mean?

Finneran

My clients will say, "Oh, you have such great ideas" or "Thank you for sharing that" or "I didn't know I could do that." And I say, "No, I'm only holding up the mirror. Everything you're doing, you've always had in you. I can see it more easily than you, because I do not share your same set of limiting beliefs, so my job is to simply reflect back to you who you actually are and what you're actually able to accomplish."

Wright

I understand you use some non-traditional coaching methods. What would some of those be?

Finneran

Yes, I do some things, which are kind of different. I ask my clients to keep track of the synchronicities they see happening in their lives and actually keep a synchronicity journal to discover how those particular coincidences may actually have a message for them. I also ask my clients to journal daily. I resisted doing this for years, even though I said I wanted to. I finally developed the habit two years ago and it is normally the first thing I do every morning. I have learned a lot about myself through those pages. I ask them to a spend time daily reading on various topics. I also have a daily message I ask them to call in and listen to where I am asking a specific question for the day and they leave their answers.

Wright

A lot of people in our audience and also reading this book will not know what synchronicity is. Could you kind of give us a layman's version of what it is?

Finneran

Absolutely, a synchronicity is when, for example, you have a friend whom you haven't seen or talked to in a period of time; they happen to pop in your mind for some reason and the next minute the phone rings and it's them.

Wright

So, what other people would call mere coincidences you think there is some connection. They're not coincidences at all but some sort of connectedness?

Finneran

I know there is a connectedness, David. Also if you look at the word coincidence, it comes from the word coincide. It's a geometry term for when two angles coincide perfectly. So, there's really nothing random about it. We've always expressed this concept as being two unrelated things, which just happen to come together, but coincide means a perfect geometric match. I look at synchronicities as road-maps keeping me going in the right direction or simply validating a decision I have already made.

Wright

Explain your belief that all coaches need to be coached.

Finneran

I tell my clients the first requirement to look for in a potential coach is to ensure the person they are considering as a coach, also has their own coach. I don't feel any of us ever have all of the answers. Coaching and being coached is a synergistic, dynamic relationship. Sometimes when I am coaching, I learn as much or more from my client as they learn from me. It is my belief as coaches; we always need to be growing, evolving and involved in the process of being coached to be an effective coach with your own clients.

Wright

Is a coach's coach the same as a mentor?

Finneran

It can be. I actually do mentor coaching for several coaches. One of my coaches whom I've been coached by for seven years is a mentor coach for me, and he also helps me look at and expand my life in new ways. When I am in the role of a mentor coach, I work specifically to help coaches develop or fine tune their coaching skills, as well as working on goals and objectives in their own lives.

Wright

How has coaching changed your life personally?

Finneran

It has allowed me to see the possibilities, which are open to me, and to understand and know I actually can live my life with purpose. It has made me a more aware person of how my actions and attitudes influence and direct my life.

Wright

Can you tell us a little bit about your husband, Kevin, whom I understand is one of your most successful coaching clients?

Finneran

Well, I would love to because it's a great story. Three years ago this month my husband, Kevin, was a bio-medical equipment technician working in a hospital operating room, about as left-brained as you can be. We were sitting out in the backyard one day and I said, "Kevin, if you didn't ever have to go back to the hospital, what would you do?" He said that he would be a painter. Now, at that time, David, we'd been married 19 years and I had never seen him paint anything other than walls. I said, "So, paint houses?" He said, "No, I'd paint pictures." I said, "You've never painted anything." "I know," he replied. "How do you know you could paint?" "I just know." I said, "Well, would people buy your paintings?" He said, "Yes." I replied, "How do you know?" And he said, "I just know." So, we sat down and figured out how many more houses I would need to sell per month to cover the income he would be giving up if he decided to do this. He was the one with the traditional job with the health insurance and the paid vacation. So, we sat there and figured it all out and Kevin never went back to the hospital. He actually gave his notice the next day and went out and bought art supplies! In fact, Kevin recently submitted his story in response to a magazine asking for stories of people who "had heeded the call of true desire."

Wright

You're kidding!

Finneran

I'm not kidding. Everyone goes, "Oh, my gosh," but he never went back to the hospital. It's three years later; he's a very successful island artist. He owns the business, Maui Maniacs. He's had several successful art shows. There was a full-page article about him in the *San Diego Business Journal,* about art as a business. Once we got his right brain ignited he started doing all sorts of things. He had his first poem published in January. He's doing graphic design right now for a new woman's surfboard company to be launched in September of this year called "Move Over Boys." I've watched a metamorphosis in this person going from one kind of life to an entirely different kind of life. What I love about Kev's story is when I have clients tell me, "Well, I can't do that, I have responsibilities," I say, "Don't tell Kevin. Don't tell Kevin you can't live the life of your dreams, because he is living the life of his dreams."

Wright

It sounds like it.

Finneran

It's so exciting to watch and to be a part of making it happen.

Wright

Could you share some other success stories of your clients?

Finneran

Absolutely. In fact, one of the favorite quotes on my web site comes from me. It says, "I feel like I'm in the eye of a hurricane with all of my amazing clients swirling around me ready to blow everything and everyone away with their magnificence." I had a client, Celeste, who was a realtor and couldn't stand her job. Now she has an opportunity for ghost writing a book about a man who escaped from Afghanistan when he was 16 years old. So, she's gone from being a realtor and hating it to on the road to becoming a great author. I have another client who hated being a realtor but just needed to change her attitude. Kathy will be one of Richmond's number one realtors very shortly, without a doubt and is already one of the top producers in her office. I have a client who is transitioning from a Account Manager position, traveling a great deal of the time, to working with animals, which has always been Melinda's dream. My client Karen has a global vision and mission, involved in with Indigo Children. It's just amazing.

Wright

It certainly is. Explain your moment of knowing that everything happens for a reason.

Finneran

Well, that was a tough moment, but what happened is, I had decided several years ago to become a minister for the Church of Religious Science. So, for three years, I dedicated everything in my life to accomplishing that dream. I went back to school and completed my bachelor's degree in record time. I was taking six and seven classes at a time and also taking practitioner classes at church.

Finally the moment arrived when it was time for me to have my oral interview for admission to ministerial school. I went to the interview and there were three people interviewing me. From the moment I entered, I felt my intuition telling me something wasn't right. The result of the interview was the panel felt I was rushing my path too much; they wanted me to wait a year before starting ministerial school. I remember leaving there crying and crying because this was what I had devoted the last three years of my life to attaining and in twenty minutes it was gone. As I was driving away, I said, "Okay, God, here is the test. If I truly believe everything happens for a reason, this must be what is meant to be." So, the test was, do I believe this or not, and my answer was yes. While I was extremely disappointed and I didn't understand why the one thing I had been working on so determinedly had been denied to me, in retrospect it just makes such perfect sense. Within a month following the denial of admission to ministerial school, my newsletter *Dharma Pathways* was launched and it has since doubled in circulation. Also my coaching business really took off and my speaking engagements have increased. I now realize the path I had set for myself, as a minister was really not broad enough to encompass everything I wanted to do.

Wright

Describe the type of clients that you enjoy working with.

Finneran

I like clients who are open-minded, who enjoy my kind of kooky sense of humor, who are willing to look at new perspectives, and who are totally honest; that's a very important requirement. Also, I like clients who want to make a difference in their life and in other people's lives and who are ready to commit and excited about taking the next step.

Wright

So, what is the vision that you have for your business?

Finneran

I envision my business expanding tremendously. At some point, I see having a number of coaches working with me to enlarge the personal coaching side of the business because I would really like to expand the speaking side. People say, "What do you really see as your mission?" and I say, "I see myself as the S.S.U." That is the Spiritual Speaker of the Universe. I would like to travel all over the world to talking to people, to show them how all of their amazing, unused potential is sitting there waiting for them to discover it. So, I see—this may sound like a pretty big plan—but I see myself working to help raise spiritual consciousness and the ability of human potential throughout the world.

Wright

What do you hope your clients will achieve as a result of working with you?

Finneran

The main thing I want is for each of them to have an unshakeable belief in themselves, to understand they are perfect, whole, and complete and their number one priority is taking care of themselves and going for their dreams; knowing they are here for a divine purpose.

Wright

With all of our *Conversations on Success* books, we're trying to find people who will be a good role model to go into our books and can help our readers and audience to be better, you know, to become better, to be happier, to be more successful, just by their example. Is there anyone in your life that has made a real difference and made you a better person?

Finneran

Absolutely. Number one I would have to say my husband, Kevin, who has always been a role model of role models for unconditional love and support. He has taught me what's inside a person is what is important, who the person really is. He has truly demonstrated his belief in the 22 years we've been married. So, Kevin would be my number one role model. A second one would be my coach, Tim, who I said I've worked with for the last seven years. Tim is someone else who has expressed unconditional support and 100 percent commitment and belief in me. When I am describing my coaching skills, I proudly say, "I was trained by the best there is." Having Tim as my coach has contributed to who I am today. The third would be my mom. Growing up my mom worked for the County of Orange. She started working for the county as a clerical person and ended up in a very high management position in the Tax Collector's office. She created and designed each of those jobs for herself as she went up the career ladder. As a result, I never felt, as a woman, I didn't have just as much opportunity as anyone else. So, I would say those are the three most important role models in my life.

Wright

Very interesting. Well, Judi, this has been educational for me today. I've learned a lot and I really do appreciate you taking this time with me.

Finneran

I am happy and excited to be a part of *Conversations on Success*.

Wright

Today we have been talking to Judi Finneran. She has been speaking professionally for over 20 years and as we have found out today she provides useful tools and ideas to allow people in her audiences to put the knowledge into practice immediately to create the change that they are looking for in their lives. Judi, thank you so much for being with us.

Finneran

David, it was my pleasure, thank you very much.

About The Author

With 20 years of inspiring audiences as a professional speaker, coach & author, Judi evokes the best of the human spirit. Whether sitting in the audience during one of her presentations, experiencing one-on-one coaching or reading her motivational writings, Judi helps you recognize your gifts and bring them forth: to fulfill your life mission. Judi's success as a top-producing realtor, paved the way to her current coaching career. She founded Dharma Coaching in 2001 and is a Certified Dream Coach.™

Judi Finneran
Dharma Coaching
PO Box 130153
Carlsbad, California 92013
Website: www.dharmacoachingpath.com

Chapter 14

JOSEPH MANCUSI, PH.D.

THE INTERVIEW

David E. Wright (Wright)

Today we are talking to Joseph Mancusi. Dr. Mancusi has been called "One of America's most inspirational speakers." Dr. Mancusi's company specializes in taking people to the next level. He engages in organizational development, team building, stress and change management, corporate culture change, cultural diversity, leadership development, and employee training. The American Psychological Association (APA) considers him a subject matter expert. As such, he is referred by the APA to the media. He is frequently called upon as an expert in the psychology of the work place, stress at work, men and women at work, and the psychology of soldiers and veterans. At the Veterans Administration he directed the largest psychology program in the world with 1400 doctoral psychologists in 171 hospitals and 350 clinics. He made frequent visits to the VA Medical Centers to assess the effectiveness of the psychological and mental health services. He was the principal interagency contact for psychological services. In this capacity, he made presentations at the annual meeting of the American Psychological Association and other academic organizations. Dr. Mancusi, welcome to *Conversations on Success.*

Joseph Mancusi (Mancusi)

Well, thank you. I am delighted to be here.

Wright

Dr. Mancusi, you have a Bachelor's Degree and a Master's Degree in chemistry and biochemistry. How did you ever end up with a Ph.D. in clinical psychology from Duke?

Mancusi

Well, I think that's a good question. Everybody wonders about that. I started out to be a medical doctor and ran out of money. So, after my Bachelor's Degree in chemistry, I was offered a fellowship at Iowa State University to get a Ph.D. in biochemistry. However, I was not happy with my choice. I went to see a psychologist after about a year and a half and tried to answer, "What do I really need to do in my life?" I took some tests at Iowa State in the counseling department and the answer came back, "You know, you're probably good at chemistry, but you don't have the personality for it. Your personality is a better fit for psychology." I had never taken a psychology course up until that time. I took a few psychology courses, I loved them, and I ended up going to Duke. So, many people stay in a field they are good at, even when they don't like what they are doing. People should find what they are good at and what they love doing. I was on my way to being successful and unhappy. But that is not success.

Wright

With everything else you do, you are also an expert on safety. How in the world did you get into that field?

Mancusi

I got into the field of safety by telling a large utility that I did not do training in safety. When people ask me to do training I have three answers for them. Yes, I do it; no, I don't; or I'll find out. When Con Edison, one of the largest electrical companies in the United States called me, I said "I don't teach safety." They called me back about a week later and they begged me to try to do a safety program for them, a daylong program for 1,000 employees, 100 at a time. Again, I said, "I don't do safety." Finally, they called me a third time. They said, "Look, we know about electrical safety. We want your style of talking to people. We want the way you teach. We want to change our corporate culture using safety. We want to build teams. Our executives have seen you and know you are good at changing corporate culture and building teams." Sometimes people will push you or pull you to your destiny. They see things in you that you don't see. This was an example in my life. We must be open to see the good things in ourselves that others see. So, I went to the Internet, that is a great source, and pulled out 600 articles, looked at 300 of them closely, and now I have a three-day program on safety, health, and the environment. They wanted my ability to communicate with the ordinary person. They didn't want my Ph.D., they wanted me.

Wright

So, facilitation is what they really needed, huh?

Mancusi

Exactly, they needed somebody who would teach safety in a way that could change their corporate culture. The utility had about 15 thousand people at the time, and we ended up having a 35 percent drop in accidents as a result of putting on training programs. The team became the unit responsible for safety, along with the worker. It was so satisfying to see that people's eyes, fingers, arms and backs were saved. It is like curing people without the need for medical treatment.

Wright

Wow!

Mancusi

We concentrated on making people responsible for each other, not the boss responsible for them. Now workers would tell each other to put on the hard hat. We work smart around here. They didn't wait for management to catch the workers. The workers themselves became responsible for safety and each other. As a result of my "new career" in safety, I have given talks at governor's conferences in Alaska, Alabama and Oregon. I have spoken on safety at NASA. Opportunity knocked three times and I almost told it "No" three times.

Wright

Is it true that you didn't get on the Phil Donohue show because of Gorbachev, the Prime Minister of USSR?

Mancusi

Yes, I always wanted to be on the Phil Donohue show, and it was all scheduled and ready to go. Somehow, unexpectedly, Gorbachev ended up in the United States. The producer of Donahue called me and said, "We'll schedule you later! But Gorbachev is more important than you," That almost broke my heart. I'm a casualty of the Cold War. It was such a great opportunity, the opportunity went away, and they never invited me back because Donohue went off the air soon after. It really taught me a lesson. If you get an opportunity, go for it before it's taken away because Gorbachev may just be lurking in the wings somewhere. Don't wait for the second opportunity to come. Seize the first one.

Wright

You were in charge of 1400 Ph.D. psychologists in 171 medical centers and 350 clinics for the Veterans Administration. How did it feel to have that many psychologists just a phone call away?

Mancusi

Well, it's scary to know that there are that many folks who can pick up the line. In fact, my boss said that I should never give them my direct phone number. He said that they should always talk to the secretary first. But I believe that the way to stop a bureaucracy is to be accessible yourself. So, I took all phone calls from veterans and psychologists directly if I was available. It saved time and was more personable. I'm so glad I did. I only got calls two from veterans. I helped one veteran get admitted to the hospital, and the other I held on the phone because he was threatening to attempt suicide. I kept on talking to him while my secretary notified people who could locate where he was. I encourage presidents of companies to give their number out. People will rarely call the top boss, but when they do, it can save a lot of trouble. That kind of intimate contact is so important. One president of a large insurance company that I know writes 10 to 20 birthday cards a day. He has to send out over 7,000 a year to his employees, customers, and friends. It is still a thrill for an employee after 20 years to get a hand signed card with a comment on it from the president of the company. The first President Bush used to leave parties at night at the White House and spend at least a half an hour writing thank-you notes to people who had helped him. A client of mine gave President Bush a set of Horseshoes. Five years later President Bush sent him a note telling him that he was still using them. People never forget things like that. It makes their day and it makes them want to make yours. So, I told the psychologists, "Give me a call." Unfortunately not very many of them did.

Wright

You wonder why.

Mancusi

Well, I think they are afraid of bothering you and they are intimidated. They also are now part of the bureaucracy that they complain about. I did have one problem psychologist. He called me three times in the first three months, and he said, "You know, I've only called you three times in three months." He didn't have anything of importance to talk about. He was trying to butter up the boss. And I told him, "If all 1400 people had called me, I would have had 4200 phone calls." He never called me again.

Wright

You have given speeches around the world—New Zealand, Argentina, France, Holland, the Soviet Union, and the White House six times. What was the most unusual situation you found?

Mancusi

Well, it would be easy to say the White House was the most unusual just because not very many people get to speak there. They had me back six times. By the way, I never slept in the Lincoln bedroom. You know, you're checked by security when you go into the White House and you're checked again when you go into a room that the President may enter. I also did a talk, several talks in fact, on Johnston Atoll, an island that is 600 miles from any other human beings. It's out in the Pacific about 800 miles from Hawaii, and they dispose of chemical weapons there. The island is only two miles long. One part has thousands of weapons, another section has leftover Agent Orange, and another section had radioactive residue leftover when a rocket exploded on the pad years earlier. When I got off the plane, I was the only one getting off, and they gave me a gas mask. They made me test the gas mask, and they gave me these two little canisters that look like magic markers that contained antidotes for the two types of gas weapons on the island. You are supposed to stick them in your thigh if you have any symptoms of gas poisoning. One you would stick if you felt nauseous, anxious and sweaty. If you felt headachy, had trouble breathing and felt like you were going to faint, you stuck the other one in your thigh. As soon as they told me the symptoms, I said, "Can I stick them now? I'm getting all those symptoms while you're describing them to me." Only three planes a week go in or out, and they managed to lose my luggage. Also, there was no glass in the windows in the room where I was speaking so my overhead transparencies kept blowing off the projector. I would have to say that that Johnston Atoll was the most unusual place I've ever spoken.

Wright

You have spoken at the White House six times, in New Zealand, Argentina, France, Holland, and Soviet Union. You've spoken at a sewage plant, on an island where they dispose of biological weapons and at some of the best resorts in the world. I know you grew up poor and once slept four brothers in the same bed. How does someone go from poverty with no hot water, no shower, no tub, to the White House? What can you teach other people about success?

Mancusi

1. Don't let other people discourage you.

Well, I'll tell you the first thing is don't let other people discourage you. Poverty is not just about money; it is about your spirit. All along people would tell me I couldn't get into college because my family didn't have money. Or I wouldn't be able to do this or that because I was too poor. These people think they are trying to help you; they want you to face the facts so you won't be too hurt. I call the things they tell you "Destructive Fantasies."

2. Follow your own Delicious Fantasies.

Only time, opportunity and your personality will determine whether or not you will succeed. You have to have "Delicious Fantasies." You have to follow your own Delicious Fantasies, and that is one of the worst things that poverty and abuse do. They destroy your "Delicious Fantasies." So, another thing I'd say is, Keep your "Delicious Fantasies," those dreams that are so good you can almost taste them. Don't let people discourage you. My own mother told me I couldn't go to college, and she made it very clear that we didn't have any money. I couldn't even sign up for college prep courses in high school where I would take the toughest math, the toughest science, and the toughest languages. She said, "You're taking Wood Shop." To my mother, real success was to be found in the three "T's"—Tools, a Trade, and a Truck. She wanted me to be a mechanic, a machinist, a painter, a carpenter, or a plumber because they all have tools, a trade, and a truck. So, that's the first thing. Don't listen to the negative people around you even if they love you. Sometimes, the closest people to you discourage you the most. My Mom left school in the sixth grade to go out and work in a factory. Her father, a coal miner died of black lung disease. Her father didn't have tools or a trade. She was trying to protect me. Luckily, for me, my mother's cousin Sarah convinced my Mom to let me take college preparatory courses. I was the only kid in high school taking machine shop and Latin at the same time.

3. Work at the same speed regardless of the pay.

Another rule is something that my Dad told me. He said always work at the same speed no matter what people pay you. Don't work half as fast for someone that gives you half the pay. Work at top speed all the time and then as you go forward, they'll say, "Hey, he's a good worker," and then you'll get better jobs. I do just as much work preparing for a free talk as I do for one that pays well.

4. Always have clear goals.

Next, I've always had clear goals, and I've always worked hard toward those goals. You know, it's the old thing. If you don't know where you're going, any road will do. You've got to be able to set those goals and to see how you're doing on it. Successful people are constantly working towards goals. Even if their goals change they know how to accomplish new goals because they have worked on old ones.

5. Stay optimistic.

Not the last point but certainly in some ways I think the most important is to stay optimistic. I spend a lot of time teaching about how to stay optimistic. Optimism may not guarantee success, but pessimism will guarantee failure. Pessimists are always right. If they say they can't do it, they can't. Pessimists will go out of their way to prove themselves right. They work harder than optimists to prove themselves right, and they can cause trouble when they are in organizations.

6. Learn from every success and failure.

You did not fail if you can take a lesson away from the experience. Thomas Edison searched the world for the best filament for the light bulb and the best plant to make rubber for tires. In fact he became an expert on plants while researching rubber plants. A reporter asked Edison how it feels to know that he failed 2000 times before he found the right filament for the light bulb. Edison replied that he did not fail 2000 times; he found 2000 ways that do not work. He learned something from every non-success and, thus did not fail. That kept his unquenchable thirst for knowledge going.

Wright

You spend a lot of time talking and writing about optimists. Is the research really clear about the effect of optimism on one's life?

Mancusi

You know, it is so clear that it's a shame that we haven't paid more attention to it. It's one of the key components of what psychologists call emotional intelligence. For example, optimists are healthier. If doctors examine people who are over 65, and they take a look at the optimist versus the pessimist, the optimists have better lungs eight years later. Optimists have fewer heart attacks, survive heart attacks better and do better after heart surgery. Optimists sell more as sales people. Let me just give you a couple of examples. When you compare optimists versus pessimists, and there's a simple test you can use to find this out, the results are startling. In the automotive industry optimists outsell the pessimists by 20 percent. And optimistic sales managers outsell pessimistic managers by 27 percent. In telecommunication optimists outsell pessimists by 29 percent. In office products optimists outsell by 29 percent, and in real estate they outsell by 33 percent. Optimistic insurance agents outsell pessimists by 37 percent. Extreme optimists outsell extreme pessimists by 88 percent in the insurance field. I remember what a top real estate agent told me. Total sales in the area had gone down by 10 percent. I said, "Boy, it must be terrible to be in your business now." She said, "No, why do you say that?" I said, "Well, I know that 10 percent fewer houses are being sold." She said, "You're right. Only 10 percent less are being sold, but 60 percent of all the real estate agents have already given up. They think the market is so bad they can't make a sale." She said, "How would you like to be in a business where 60 percent of your competitors go away in bad times?" "That's what happens in bad times to most real estate agents. I love bad times." This woman was number one in her company for several years in a row. I bought my home through her.

Wright

She's absolutely right. I was in that industry in the last quarter of '79 and the first quarter of '80, and the industry went down 20 percent, which would ruin most industries. The sales figures went down. I was closing 1100 single-family dwellings at the time, which is about $150 million today, but the industry went down 20 percent, which wipes out most industries. But 50 percent of the people quit.

Mancusi

Exactly. Some people run away from trouble so fast they pass opportunity on the way out.

Wright

So, you're really selling more if you're smart enough to stick around.

Mancusi

That's right. An important question is: "Can you train someone to be optimistic?" The results are encouraging. In one study they trained very pessimistic people and they found that just by training them, they had less depression and less anxiety. Another finding is that when you train people to be optimists, they take better care of their health. They actually saw doctors more than the pessimists who were not trained. They are not afraid to look at health care information. See, if you're an optimist and someone says, "Here read about cancer," you will do it. You might say: "Okay, I'm going to read because I'll find out what I can do to prevent cancer." If you're a pessimist, you're going to say, "Nah, it won't do any good anyway," and boom— you end up dying with cancer just because you avoid looking at reality.

Wright

You appeared at the Society for Human Resource Management National Convention five times and in fact was named top speaker all five times. With hundreds of speakers at each convention, that's quite an accomplishment. I understand the audiotapes "Why Some People

In Organizations Always Succeed" and "The Emotionally Intelligent Organization" were both top sellers. Are those tapes still available for any one of our readers who might want to listen?

Mancusi

Absolutely, and they can be ordered on our website. We have two websites: www.mancusi.net or www.goodwhale.com. Folks can actually e-mail me at jmancusi@earthlink.net and we would be glad to put them in touch with our various tapes, CDs, and video presentations.

Wright

For over 20 years now you have been called Dr. Goodwhale. What's up with that unusual name?

Mancusi

Well, I've lost 40 pounds so, I'm probably not being called Dr. Goodwhale any more because of my weight. But over 20 years ago I realized that if we could train a killer whale (Orcas), we could train anybody. I looked at the characteristics of killer whales and decided that human beings who had these traits would be at the top of the food chain just like killer whales. For example, Orcas are totally team animals. Killer whales over communicate; they hear each other over 400 square kilometers of ocean. I mean every Orca hears the same message at the same time. How much better off would we be in business if teamwork and communication were spread across the organization? Orcas appear to have passion and enthusiasm, and you and I both know how people with passion and enthusiasm can be successful. Orcas have confidence in themselves. They do not back down from trouble—nor do they seek it out. They have tremendous curiosity. They are open to new ideas. They are constantly checking things out. Killer whales also do things that very few people do. They take advantage of opportunities. They will, if they see seals on the shore, learn how to go get seals off the rocks or beach. Orcas spend a lot of time—over 16 years—developing and mentoring others and teaching the young what to do. They build partnerships, they totally support the team. They consistently cope with stress. They respond very well to positive encouragement. A trainer cannot yell at a killer whale or try to force it to do anything. The only Orcas that have ever killed human beings have been in a tank. They have never killed humans that we know in the wild. Well, if we take those same tactics with people that we supervise, if we treat them fairly, if we realize that they're like killer whales. Orcas don't really work for the little bit of food we give them; they work for the attention, for the thank-you. So, when I give my talks, I point out that you can train killer whales to jump over a rope by constantly telling them "Goodwhale, Goodwhale, Goodwhale." People also can be motivated by consistency and caring. At the end of my talks I'll ask people, "How do you get Killer Whales to do two flips in the air? What happens when they do a flip?" I say, "You yell Goodwhale, Goodwhale, Goodwhale!" I also tell the audience that if you tell someone you know 'Goodwhale, Goodwhale, Good-whale!' they'll leave it in the act. Then I say, "How many of you are married?" and many raise their hands. And I say, "Well, how many of you would be better lovers if you did something right in bed and your spouse said 'Goodwhale, Goodwhale, Goodwhale'?" Every man wants to hear 'Goodwhale' once in his life. I once taught human sexuality in a medical school, so I guess I can talk about things like that.

Wright

Speaking of your presentations, your latest talk is called *"Going from Existing to Excelling."* Can you tell us a little bit about that?

Mancusi

Yes, I think that most people are never really, truly successful. They settle for just existing in the world when they could excel. It is the same for companies. Jim Collins in his book *Good to Great* has the best analysis I have seen of what it takes for a company to succeed. My analysis extends his work with observations I have made as a therapist, consultant and trainer. In order for a person to go from ex-isting to excelling, three factors must all line up together. First, you have to know what you're good at. Second, what are you really pas-sionate about? And third, what enhances your self worth? When these three factors come together it creates what I call a *Center of Excel-lence*©, and the larger the *Center of Excellence*© the greater the success you are going to have. Ask yourself some questions about your job.

What are my strengths?

What are my strengths? Are they used on the job? What am I really good at? And If I'm not good at certain things and I need to be, I need to either develop the skills or get someone else to do it for me.

What am I passionate about?

The second thing is what am I passionate about? What turns me on? Would I do my job for free if I had a million dollars? As for passion, I'll mention it in just a minute because that's what made me change careers.

Does what I do enhance my self worth?

Finally, does what I do enhance my self worth? Does it make me feel good about myself? Is my self-esteem improved? There are so many people, who are passionate about something, and they are good at it, but in fact, what they do doesn't enhance their self worth. One example is the "too busy executives." You know they're good at their jobs and they advance rapidly. They have an obvious passion about what they do, but what drives the self worth of some? The answer might be being a good parent, a good spouse, and helping other people. But they don't have time for that. Well, if you don't have time for that you won't have a big "Center of Excellence," and you're not going to be an excelling person. You are going to be stuck in just existing. Another group of people is the "Stock Manipulators." They constantly do things that they know destroys their self worth. The people who make phone calls to the elderly to get money from them are also in this category. They're good at it, and they're passionate about it, but if honesty and being a good person and helping others and caring for others are what drive their self worth, they will fail. Most people need to feel clean and good about what they do. If you don't, you are never going to be successful. When I was a biochemist, I had a fellowship at Iowa State University, and I was very proud of it. It helped my self worth. I knew I could make a living helping people by doing research on chemicals. I was good at it. Then it dawned on me, chemistry wasn't my passion anymore. I got into chemistry because I wanted to be an M.D. and not a Ph.D. chemist. I became what I call the "frustrated chemist," because what I was really passionate about is motivating people, helping others, and teaching. And unless I did that, I wasn't going to be satisfied. So, two courses short of a Ph.D. in biochemistry, I walked away from the chemistry degree and went into psychology. I didn't want to experience one of the greatest sources of pain that a person can have. That is doing something you're good at but you hate doing, and you keep doing it. We've all seen the "depressed accountant." You know, he's good at his job, and he makes money at it, but in the end, it isn't his passion. So many people are miserable in life because they end up good at something that they hate doing and they keep on doing it.

Wright

I've heard and read statistics as high as 87 percent of all Americans get up in the morning and go to a place they don't want to be.

Mancusi

Thank you. That is a terrific point. You're absolutely right; it's a place they don't want to be with people they don't want to be with. You don't always get a chance to do what you're passionate about however. I have a friend of mine that wanted to be an artist. Being around art and artists increased his self worth. He felt special. He was passionate about his art. Sadly he was good at almost anything except art. So, he was never successful. I call him the "Starving Artist." Now what's interesting about him was that he suffered because his passion was art, and he would never be an accomplished artist. He just didn't have the talent. Well, guess what he does now? He's an art dealer, and he has discovered that what he is best at is selling art. You know one of life's greatest joys is to discover talents that were hidden from you or to help others discover theirs. So, now I call him the "happy art dealer".

Wright

Can you give our readers and our listeners some examples of people who are almost there but never quite make it, the people who just exist but don't really excel at life?

Mancusi

Yeah, I think of the person that's the starving artist or depressed accountant that I have already mentioned, and even me at one time. Anyone who is not at the same time good at what he does, passionate about it and gets high self-esteem from his job is in trouble. Most people don't find activities where all three aspects come together. I met an electrical worker who hated his job. But he was happy and this puzzled me. The job supported his real passion; raising gold fish. They are called Koi. He owned one that was worth $25,000. He took trips to Japan to enter his fish in shows and contests. His job provided the money for him to pursue his passion. Other passionless people, just as talented, sit around drinking beer or gambling with their money. I was once in a situation where I was making myself miserable. I was never able to be on the track team in high school or college because I had to work after school. When I turned 25 years old I practiced running on my own. Eventually, I ran a 5 minute and 25 second mile. Not too bad for someone who was never able to participate in track. Well, years later, I decided at age 45 to get back to running. What was my passion? Running. What will drive my self worth? To run a 5 minutes and 25 second mile at age 45 like I did when I was 25 years old. What was I good at when I was 45? Almost anything but running! I ended up hurting myself, I pulled a hamstring. I went to the doctor and he said, "Well, you can't do this running thing, you know. You have the wrong body and you're too fat, your spine and knees are not going to take the pounding." I said, "Okay," and I went away for a year. Next year I went back to stretching and I started running again because I wanted to get down to a 5 minute and 25 second mile. However, I hurt myself again. The doctor again told me not to resume running. But I didn't listen. I hurt myself trying to run the third year, and he finally said to me, "Joe, what are you trying to do?" and I said, "I'm trying to run a 5 minute and 25 second mile." He said, "No you're not. You're trying to put my kid through college." He said, "Look, if you saw somebody on the second story of a building and he yelled I'm flying and he jumped and broke a leg, and the second year you heard them yell "I'm flying, I'm flying" and he broke two legs, and the third year you saw him on the fourth story of a building and he was about to jump and he's yelling "I'm flying, I'm flying" would you say he is trying to fly or he's crazy?" I said, "He's crazy." The doctor said, "Well, you're crazy, too." He said, "Why don't you stop trying to run like a 25 year old, and why don't you just try to be the healthiest 48 year old man you can be. He was right. I was hurting myself because of a poorly set goal. Another source of pain is never to realize the limits of your ability and to keep on trying. We've all seen women and men who go in for all kinds of surgery so they can try to capture the look they had years ago and instead they look like stretched out balloons.

Wright

Right.

Mancusi

No matter how much surgery, they will never be truly happy. What is happiness? How can you tell who is truly happy? Psychologist Dr. Martin Seligman has studied happiness extensively. There are three types of happy lives. The first type of happy life is the "Pleasant Life." This is a life where we seek pleasure. It is found in the Hollywood image of satisfying all our desires. However, what do you do after the third Rolex? Where do you put it? The "Pleasant Life" is having as many pleasures as possible, eating in the best restaurants, doing all the greatest things, and after a while, you know you're not happy any more doing that.

The second type of life is the "Good Life." The "Good Life" is obtained when you know what your signature strengths are and craft your life, your work, your love, and friendship to get more flow in your life, to feel better about yourself. Well when I became a psychologist, I had the "Good Life" because I could help people and I was crafting my life, my work, and friendship to get more flow in my life and to do what I enjoyed doing. However the people who sustain happiness the longest experience the "Meaningful Life." The "Meaningful Life," however, is using your signature strength in the service of something you believe is larger than yourself. The people, who have a meaningful life, even if they get cancer, even if they get setbacks, end up still being happy because they believe in God, a greater power, family, friends, society, and the environment. They believe and work for something bigger than themselves. What they do is craft their life so that they can take care of something bigger than themselves. If you're a parent, it's easy. You can take care of your kid because you're taking care of the future, but a lot of times on the job, we don't do a good job of telling people why our company is important and how it goes beyond just making money for stockholders and stakeholders. A caring company will teach people how their work affects the world for the better. We don't give people a chance to learn what Dr. Seligman calls the "Meaningful Life".

Wright

In one of your talks you mentioned that some of the most successful people are addicts, and I know you've treated drug addicts and alcohol addicted people. Most people think of them as weak, but do you really think they are powerful?

Mancusi

Well, I'll tell you, addicts will do things we wouldn't do. They are seen as out of control, but in fact they are in control. They'll stay out all night on a rainy night or a cold night waiting for that hit of drugs. They will focus their entire life on getting that hit. Sometimes we can't focus our life on losing five pounds. We can't turn down a piece of pizza or a dish of spaghetti. But when addicts have their goals, they go after their goals, relentlessly. I looked at addicts and I realized that addicts would do almost anything to get their goals. So what I decided to tell people is to look at the fact that they need to get addicted to something. If they could be addicted and have the persistence of an addict then they are going to succeed. Very few addicts, whether they're drinkers, smokers, or drug addicts, very few of them ever go very long without meeting their goal of getting what they want into their system. They are in total control. They really care only about getting their goals met. I think it would be nice if a lot of people who struggle to succeed would just say, "Well, wait a minute. What can I be addicted to? What turns me on? And is there any way that I can then consistently work toward one end?"

Wright

You talk about five keys to success. Could you expand on that for us?

Mancusi

Vision, Values, Action, Attitude, Connections

Yes, I really feel very strongly that there are five important keys to success. The first key is your **vision**. Do you know where you want to go, you know. Someone says to me, "Am I successful?" Well where are you trying to get to go? Where are you? So, many people just don't even form a vision of where they want to go. They don't create the ideal. They don't play with their "Delicious Fantasies."

The second thing after vision is your **values**. Will your values take you to your vision? Will you be satisfied when you get there? You can have the right vision, but if you don't have the right values, you're not going to put in the time or you're not going to make the contacts, or you're not going to do what human beings who are successful do.

The third key to success is your **actions**. Do you act to ensure success and eliminate failure? Do you do what it takes in a timely manner?

The fourth key to success is **attitude**. Do you reject psychological blocks left over from the past or imposed by others? That attitude part almost caused me to fail. I was still hearing my mother say, "We're poor, you can't do it." I'd still hear my father say, "You know, you're not smart enough." As a therapist, I'd still hear clients listening to voices of the past tell them what they can't do. When I had patients in therapy, that attitude factor would come in because they would have this whole litany of what I call "Destructive Fantasies" that they carry within themselves left over from other people. They become puppets of other peoples' "Destructive Fantasies."

The fifth key to success I just put in a few years ago, and that's **connections**. Connections is the ability to establish strong ties and relationships with people, the ability to communicate, to have friends, to let others help you, and for you to help them. So, the five keys are vision, do you know where you want to go? Your values, will your values take you there? Action, do you act to ensure success? Attitude, do you stop letting psychological blocks from the past keep you down? And then finally connections, are you able to establish relationships with people?

Wright

You teach thousands of executives and company presidents. What message do you have for these leaders?

Mancusi

I think one of the key messages for executives is to make sure that you respect, care about and work with people. Treat them ethically. Teach them the greater purpose of what they do. The stonemason is just as important as the architect. We have so many people whose companies don't do well and they don't know why. Ten to 30 percent of the productivity of people is destroyed because of bad management and bad attitudes. You know it's interesting. We would never let someone come in and destroy 30 percent of our computer capacity by kicking in the computer, and yet we let supervisors and managers psychologically kick in people. We psychologically kick them and treat them poorly and nobody says anything about it because, you know, he's the boss or he's the supervisor. I think that the key issue for me in being a good executive is to have the right business vision and the values. You must care for people and convey that caring to them. We need to develop more of a caring attitude at work. It is not a dog eat dog world. Dogs do not eat dogs. We would never let people treat equipment the way we let bosses treat other people.

Wright

When you give surveys to companies, you say that there are only three very important questions to ask. What are they and why only three?

Mancusi

Well, I started out with 25 questions because I got paid by the question, and I went to work for an insurance company that gave me 100 more. So, now I had 125 questions to send out and people could fill out the forms. Over the years I started to get smarter and I realized that 90 percent of everything you need to know about a company could be found from only three questions.

Question number one: "My immediate supervisor is always interested in listening to new ideas."

If you are interested in listening to new ideas, guess what? We get innovation. We get change. We get respect for the person because I respect you enough to ask you for your ideas. If I don't want your ideas, then you're not going to take an interest in my company. You're not really going to care; you're just going to go through the motions. I find out now that I've done some testing that somewhere between 25 and 60 percent of employees say, "My boss does not want my ideas." That's like throwing away the brains of a third to two thirds of all the workers we have. How are we going to get innovation and change?

The second question is: "My immediate supervisor always gives enough praise for my work."

People ask, "What's enough praise?" Well, what's "enough"?" Enough praise is whatever the person needs. We don't put the water out for the dog on a 95 degree day on Monday and then when the water is gone, we don't say to them, "Well, I gave you water on Monday, what do you want, some today? That's all we give. We give water at the beginning of the week." So many times people will say, "Well I pay you, isn't that praise?" No, that's not praise. With praise, you build a good relationship with me. You give me a pat on the back. You make me feel good about myself. And I'm more willing to work for you because people ultimately work for recognition, as you know.

The third question is: "I trust my immediate supervisor." That is the key question.

Without trust, we don't believe anything a manager says. Without trust, we're going to watch our back. Without trust, we're going to be anxious all the time. And without trust, I will never develop a team spirit. I'm always going to wonder when you're going to stick the knife in, when you're going to do me in. So, those three questions I ask employees. I just send out three question surveys now. My immediate supervisor is always interested in listing to new ideas, my immediate supervisor gives enough praise for my work, and finally, I trust my immediate supervisor. If 10 percent don't trust, it's not too bad because one in ten isn't too bad, 90 percent are still pulling. But when you get into about 30 percent negative, that means every time you get 10 people together, three are going to run the boss down and the other seven will not defend the boss.

Wright

What an interesting conversation. I hate that we've run out of time. I could listen all day. I'm learning even as we speak. I really do appreciate the time that you have spent with me today. I certainly think that our readers and our listeners are going to learn a lot from this conversation. Today we've been talking to Joseph Mancusi. Dr. Mancusi's company specializes in organizational development, team building, change and management, stress, work place effectiveness, strategic planning, leadership development and employee training. And as we have found out this afternoon, he knows a lot about all of those things. Thank you very much, Dr. Mancusi, for being with me today.

Mancusi

David, it's my pleasure and if I've helped one person by talking a little bit about my life, it makes my day. I love the book series and I love what you are trying to do with it.

Wright

Thank you, sir.

About The Author

Dr. Joseph Mancusi is a clinical psychologist, inspirational speaker and consultant. He presented at the White House six times, in 50 states and 14 countries, The NBC Today Show, and CNN. President Reagan gave him a Presidential Commendation. He has gone from sleeping four brothers in one bed to presenting talks in a palace. Through solid information and stories about life, he brings audiences to their feet with laughter, tears, and renewed commitment to goals. He directed 1400 Ph.D.'s. for the VA. He is president of the Center for Organizational Excellence.

Joseph L. Mancusi, Ph.D.

President

Center for Organizational Excellence, Inc.

47173 Timberland Place

Sterling, Virginia 20165

Phone: 703.444.5673

Fax: 703.444.3974

Email: jmancusi@earthlink.net

Website: www.mancusi.net

Website: www.goodwhale.com

Chapter 15

KAREN LUND

THE INTERVIEW

David E. Wright (Wright)

Today we are talking to Karen Lund. As a productivity and profitability strategist, Karen Lund has 25 years experience working with companies to improve their bottom line. Karen has completed consulting projects in over 100 industries in both the United States and the Pacific Rim. She has worked with all kinds of businesses from tiny startups to large multi-nationals, always focusing on helping the organization overcome the real obstacles and seize the opportunity. Her desire to help improve organizations has led her to focus on many of the people issues of productivity. One issue is how senior leaders lead without passion, and she sees a direct correlation to lost productivity. Karen is currently doing extensive research on passion and its role in leadership, and she writes a column, "Profiles in Passion." Karen, welcome to *Conversations on Success*.

Karen Lund (Lund)

Thank you.

Wright

When you think about success what comes to mind?

Lund

How a person looks at success has to be defined by the individual. As we grow up we received messages from the media, society, culture and our families as to what success is. This perceived success could very often lead us on a path for years that may not be truly "us." The key questions for each to ask are: What is success to me? Today, I say, to me success is: What gives my life meaning, where I want to expend time and energy, and how I ensure my passion is being manifested in a meaningful way.

With this view of success I can do a number of things and will consider myself successful where the media, society or culture may say, that is really not success. And then think of this statement: Failure leads to Success. I believe this idea is another key component to success. Failure has such a negative contention to most and yet we will all experience some failure. How this relates to success is how one handles the failure. Does this devastate a person or it is a learning experience? Again, the individual decides how to look at failure. For me, all failures have been learning experiences. People should listen to their heart and look at themselves and decide what success and failure is for them.

Wright

Does it incorporate personal goals?

Lund

Personal goals are always incorporated in success, as success should not be defined just in career or job objectives. Success should encompass the entire self and be built on one's value system. If you believe that it's important to give back to the community and you find a way to do that, then you're successful.

Wright

I remember when I started in business, I went to a leadership conferences on success. Their definition was: "A progressive realization of your own personal worthwhile predetermined goals." I've used that definition for a long time.

Lund

I like it. I think when you work with people around this issue of success, they often are defining success by other people's definition. It's not a personal thing. I think that's what gets in the way of people feeling successful because they haven't defined it for themselves as you learned in that leadership conference.

Wright

How did your childhood contribute to your value system development and then allow you to become an adventure.

Lund

I grew up in Minot, North Dakota of all places. What's interesting is we really had what I call the Midwest values. Family, community, and church were the focus of my life. Even though I grew up in a small town, I mean compared to the world, the town was only about 20,000 but in North Dakota, Minot was the third largest "city." All of us growing up in that town had a city attitude or mindset. I think that mindset came as a result of growing up in an environment that was safe, encouraged a lot of learning, and got us involved in the community. Family was important. We worked. We had opportunities. This atmosphere helped me develop independence and the need to venture and experience life.

Wright

What role did education have in your life?

Lund

It was never a thought that I wouldn't go to school. It was just part of the normal routine. It allowed me an opportunity to be active. I always took part in lots of activities and learned so much: organizing, interacting with other, setting directions, and solving problems. That really started my leadership development. I attended Minot State Teachers College (now a university). The education provided me with great skills and I realized after a couple of years if I got my degree I could leave North Dakota. I was ready to venture beyond and experience other ways of life.

Wright

Leave the cold weather?

Lund

I guess so. I had no experiences except winters of cold weather. I had heard there were places that never had snow. With my young mind and willingness to experience new things I just knew there was more for me. It was time for me to leave. I really became a vagabond and I have just wandered through life enjoying all the opportunities I have had. Especially those place that had little or no snow.

Wright

You've had a number of careers. How did you use each of these careers to build toward the work you do now?

Lund

What I have found working with people for years is they often don't give themselves credit for all of their experiences, paid, volunteer, educational, and just for fun. I've always focused on 'lets look at each of your experiences'. Because these experiences, even if they weren't the best, certainly gave you opportunities to learn. I often use my story to show the impact that my seven or eight different careers have had on my personal development. I've taken each one and looked at the skills and knowledge that I had gained.

To give you an idea, I was trained to be a teacher. There are skills that I had learned in teaching that relate directly to business. As a teacher you have to define a yearly program, design how you are going to educate by setting goals and objectives, determine how to measure performance, and then deal with the students that don't perform. If you think about it, those are all critical in a business world. When I was teaching I didn't realize that what I was doing was preparing for business, but it certainly provided me with great skills.

Another career I had was as a recreation director in military hospitals for the American Red Cross. Working with the American Red Cross, most of the work was done by volunteers, and I think that's where I really learned about managing people. I learned that volunteers have the same needs as every worker in any workforce. Volunteers have a need to know what their jobs are, to be trained, to be told how effective they are, and where they can improve. They also need to be provided with challenges. And that's exactly what you need to do with every person you pay. The only difference is you never pay a volunteer with dollars.

My first exposure to profit was in property management. And then I started working as a consultant for an international consulting company. I was with them for 15 years and developed my skills and knowledge to analyze a business, identify where opportunities for improvement exist, determine what techniques should be use to make the improvements, and then how to work with everyone in an organization to help them be successful and realize the productivity increases. Skills and knowledge are usually a necessary development to realize our success. I know for me, not only has this development been fun and challenging but all my career experiences have helped me identify what brings meaning to my life and I am doing things that help me manifest my passion. Everyone can look at their various life experiences and identify all the positive aspects and clearly decide how their success will be manifested.

Wright

You did a lot of traveling with the international consulting company. In researching for this interview, I think I read that you had spent time in Singapore, Malaysia, Hong Kong, Canada, Australia, and New Zealand.

Lund

Yes, and what opportunities I have had. Working with the consulting firm my first assignment outside of the United States was Asia where I worked in Singapore, Malaysia and Hong Kong. Later I moved to Australia and also covered New Zealand. My last assignment outside of the United States was Canada. Early in my life I spent two years in Guam while working for the American Red Cross. This was during Vietnam and I really expected to go there. I would never give up all these opportunities for living and learning about other countries and cultures. I know they have made me a better person.

Wright

As you went from culture to culture, were there any characteristics about success, or the way people thought of success that were in common, or are we just really diverse?

Lund

Again I think success is often defined by culture and society and it can be totally different than how we in the western world might define success. Further, you will see success manifested in different ways. For instance, in Asia, I have never worked with such hard working people, a true definition of success for them. When I went to Asia with a startup unit, I had to hire professional staff and they worked hard and were so committed. They saw success as being totally dedicated to the organization. In Asia individual success is always tied to the family, which meant working toward achieving something better for the family unit.

Whereas, in Australia it was, "Well, we'll work on that tomorrow. Let's have fun today." The Australians were not as outward about success but they are great people, enjoy life and have a good time. They are not as driven in the same way that Asians' or even some Westerners' are. Within all these cultures you do see a difference in how success is defined. Today the influence of media has greatly impacted how the young look at success differently than the older generations. Americans have this idea that citizens from other countries would consider living in the United States to be a high level of success. Yet many of these citizens are so proud of their country and certainly don't see this as the ultimate success. Today the distinction of success between cultures is blurring.

Wright

From your many experiences, what has been the common theme? In other words, what values have become important to you?

Lund

I think the most common theme in all of this for me was the opportunity for continuous learning. I believe it's so important to keep learning. Sometimes, people get the idea when you're finished with education you stop. My experiences have allowed me to work in a hundred different industries including manufacturing, mining, banking, food processing, various service organizations and government to name a few. I'm always going into something new, but very quickly it relates to a previous experience. Learning to me is important because it keeps me young, energetic and constantly looking at things differently.

A second common theme for me has been to help people be successful. That's been my personal motto for many years: Help people be successful, again, however they define success. As I worked with people in different cultures and industries, I've tried helping them define what they want, what's important to them and how could they manifest their desires.

A third and very important theme is to respect each individual, their background, their culture and their experiences. An example of respecting people's cultural beliefs is the experience I had working in Asia. I was working for an American company, and American companies tend at times to be arrogant and think they know it all. I studied the culture before I moved there. When I arrived I asked lots of questions. How do you do this? How do you look at this? I wanted to understand what they thought and how they looked at things. It wasn't necessary for me to impose my values or my way of doing things. I first had to learn about them culturally, socially and politically. I then had to help them understand the principles of the consulting company and show the principles did not conflict with their cultural values. In Asia, one of the things I learned was you cannot allow people to lose face. I didn't understand the value because in the Western world we just confront people, boom! Well, in Asia, you cannot allow them to lose face. I had to find a way to still deal with certain issues but in a way that fit the culture. I think this approach is important whether we work with different cultures in our country or we look at how the cultures exist around the world. We really need to respect people for themselves and for their culture.

Wright

What is your life's philosophy and how has that guided you?

Lund

My life's philosophy is a holistic approach to life. That means dealing with the entire self: mentally, physically, emotionally and spiritually. And I say whatever gives me meaning is important. That's the way I operate. I really try to focus on what's important for my commitments and me. Those are the things I choose to do.

Wright

I hate the phrase "Thank God it's Friday".

Lund

I agree.

Wright

You know that confuses people who love what they do in their work.

Lund

That's right this goes back to the discussion we had on what is success. I believe you should use your time and effort anyway that makes you feel good and gives you meaning. I work, have fun, read, enjoy my family and whatever else I choose when I want to. You're right, I don't like to see people miserable all week thinking the weekend will have more to offer them.

Wright

You seem to have a strong commitment to people. How did this come about and how does it relate to your business today?

Lund

My commitment to people started when I became a teacher. Because I was responsible for educating children I realized the need to understand and communicate with each individual. As I moved through my different life experiences, I came to realize how important people are. And yet, people are regarded in such a negative manner. It seems people love to gossip, complain about their bosses, spouses and children, and often focus on negatives. Our mindset needs to shift from this negative approach about people to positive thinking. I continually see this behavior impact so many organizations as I work as a consultant and professional speaker.

Take this statement that management so often uses: "People are our greatest asset." And yet when I visit the work environment, study the corporate culture, and observe the management process I often discover something totally different. An example is when a corporate strategic plan makes reference to the development of the staff but the realization of this at the department level can be so haphazard. The management process can be very punitive and management just doesn't challenge their people. Organizations don't see that people have a greater value to an organization than just doing a piece of work. The question an organization should ask themselves is: "How are we going to maximize our human potential?" Think of human potential as about 3 yards long and yet organizations only offer a challenge to staff using 2 inches of those 3 yards.

Organizations have all this human potential that never gets utilized. I read a book a couple of years ago called, *The Other 90%*, by Robert K. Cooper. The book focuses on how to get to your other 90 percent. Managers and supervisors should read this book for insight into the concept. My commitment to people and the organization is the strong premise of my consulting business. Organizations will improve productivity by establishing the right motivational environment and find exciting ways to challenge people. Many people might and say, "Karen, you're all about softness, let's make people feel good." That is not my focus. I talk and make changes regarding people in relationship to productivity, which happens to be a hard number. What we're talking about is performance, accountability, how we challenge people, how we encourage them to grow, how we get them involved in the work, and how we make them as committed as the owner is to providing for our customers.

For me, management and leaders do not effectively handle the people issue within organizations. Senior leaders today often say the right things and probably some even believe them. But, that message and how it gets carried down to all the layers within the organization just doesn't happen effectively. I find people who aren't challenged, who don't enjoy work, who are looking for another job when the economy turns around, who gossip and bad mouth many people in the organization, and just aren't committed to the organization. This results in huge turnover and low morale.

Wright

So, what do you see as the solutions to these people issues?

Lund

There are many solutions but I see two important ones today. Leaders and manager must operate from their passion. When I define passion it is that inner core, what you really like to do, how you think and feel, what makes your happy. Some might refer to their passion as the gift they were given. The entire leadership team won't have the same passion but they should complement each other's. With the senior leadership team understanding this passion the direction of the organization will be clearer. If the messages, communication and behaviors by these leaders are consistent, everyone will understand why we do business—which is our customers and how they are to be treated. As well as the priorities for our staff so that we have a motivating and learning environment. Staff may not feel the same passion as the leaders. That's fine as long as they are not in a negative mode.

A second important solution is to train leaders, managers and supervisors on how to manage that motivating and learning environment. Some people in this group need to have a mindset change on how to deal with people in a non-punitive manner. The best workers are often promoted to supervisors and not trained. These two jobs are totally different. Training is not putting people in a classroom and conducting lectures, what is needed is helping people implement the right behaviors in the work environment. Much easier said than done.

Wright

You've been talking about passion. Would you explain the work you are doing with passion and what does it mean to your business?

Lund

Like I've explained, passion is that inner core, and I'm not sure it is fully utilized by leaders and even individuals. I know we need to find ways to maximize the human potential that we interact with each day. I have found there's a direct correlation between passion and productivity both individually and for an organization. I've interviewed a number of entrepreneurs and usually entrepreneurs can identify their passions fairly easily as that's what their business is about. When you look at larger organizations, you often find those leaders also have a passion. But the question is, how well does the organization understand the passion of the Senior Leaders?" The work I'm doing now is l helping senior leaders understand their passion and how to effectively communicate the message and then manage the outcome. I'm not saying that everybody in the organization will claim the same passion. But, I am saying if senior leaders correctly communicate that passion, and demonstrate that passion in the work they do, at least all layers within the organization will have an understanding, and they will probably make a stronger commitment to what they do. I speak on this topic in a program called "Passion, People, Profits." You can use your passion with your people and if used effectively you will improve profits.

I've done a number of interviews focusing on individuals who have a unique business, or job and appeared to like what they were doing. I'm able to identify their passion—some know immediately—and I find the story that tells how they manifest that passion. With these interviews I do a column, "Profiles in Passion," and later a book will be produced. I'll give you a quick story from one of my interviews. Here in Minnesota there are zamboni drivers. Do you know what a zamboni is?

Wright

I have no idea.

Lund

That's the machine that lays down a sheet of ice on a hockey rink. A young man from St. Paul went to the Olympics as a zamboni driver. When I heard the story I thought there's has to be a relationship to this man's passion. During the interview I found out that the National Hockey League rates all the zamboni drivers on the sheet of ice they lay down. He was in the top five zamboni drivers in the NHL and was selected to go to the Olympics to lay down the sheet of ice for the ice hockey games. In interviewing him I found out his passion wasn't driving a zamboni but his passion is doing things the best way possible. So, everything he does, he works on until it is as good as he can make it, and is currently doing this at his job as an operating manager of a major sports arena.

Wright

All of our southern readers have just learned something new. I had no idea what a zamboni was. I thought you were talking about a magician like in "The Great Zamboni".

Lund

I know there are hockey teams in the south. Wherever you've got to put a sheet of ice down, there has to be a zamboni. This story shows that, that deep inner core of passion will be manifested in various ways throughout one's life. I interview people weekly in order to discover exactly how individuals see their passion and find out about their various experiences. My study of organizations is to determine how to effectively use passion in managing the organization.

Wright

What an enlightening conversation. I really do appreciate you being with us today.

Lund

Thank you.

Wright

We have been talking today to Karen Lund. She is a productivity and profitability strategist, she has 25 years of experience, and as we have found out today, a very, very intellectual look at this thing called success. Thank you so much for being with us.

About The Author

As a productivity and profitability strategist, Karen Lund has 25 years experience working with organizations and leaders who want to impact the organization through the effective use of passion. She knows that there is a direct correlation between productivity and passion and yet organizations do not maximize their effectiveness through the use of this tool. Karen has worked with multi-nationals, government, and privately owned companies in more than 100 industries in the United States and the Pacific Rim.

Karen Lund

The Lund Group

1043 Grand Ave. #317

St. Paul, Minnesota 55105

Phone: 651.690.4148

Email: klund@minn.net

Website: www.LundConsultingGroup.com

Chapter 16

DWIGHT BROWN

THE INTERVIEW

David E. Wright (Wright)

Today we're talking to Dwight Brown. Dwight has immeasurable experience as a motivational speaker having delivered speeches to several groups. He is heavily involved with the Maranantha House and served as Vice-President and eventually as President of the Board of Directors of which he is still a member. The Department of Mental Health funds the Maranantha House. He has helped shape the overall image and mold the vision of the organization. As a public speaker, Dwight is also part of the highly coveted International Speaker's Network. Through this network he participates in a professional pool of speakers, consultants, and business trainers who conduct workshop seminars throughout the country during the year. Dwight completed a three-day intensive salesmanship course under the tutelage of North Carolina millionaire businessman, Joe Dudley, a Horatio Alger award recipient who was invited to chair a small business committee by President Bush. Dwight also has an extensive sales background and he thoroughly enjoys getting out and developing new business contacts. Dwight Brown is community involved. He has volunteered throughout Fayetteville and the surrounding communities. His past involvement includes Cumberland County Minority AIDS Speaker's Bureau, Fuller Schools Adult Disabilities, Cumberland County Shelter Workshop, and the Self-Improvement Academy demonstrate Dwight's strong community connection. Dwight, welcome to *Conversations on Success*.

Dwight Brown (Brown)
Thank you, David.

Wright
Tell us a little bit about your family.

Brown
Well, my grandmother raised me. My father, on his deathbed asked my grandmother to raise me. She raised me from the time I was a young boy and then adopted me later. My mother is still living, so I tell everybody that I have two mothers. I was able to learn a lot from my grandmother from her raising me.

Wright
Tell us a little more about your childhood.

Brown
My childhood. When I was growing up, I was an overweight, fat kid. I'm not just talking about pudgy, I'm talking about so overweight that my belly overlapped my belt. When we went shopping we would look in the "H" area for husky. I never was used to going to an area in the store for my size. I was used to going to the "H" area. It got to the point where I was sick and tired because I would get up all times of the night eating and eating and eating. During those times, I wasn't very active. Food was my sport; it was my hobby and my woman. I got sick and tired of it. I told my grandmother that I was ready to lose weight. I just made a commitment to myself and told myself that I was sick and tired of being this way. That was right before I started going to high school. The only thing I did was start eating right. I changed my junk food to food. All I did was change my habits. I started walking some and I got down in a few months, to a regular size and have stayed that way ever since.

Wright
That's great. I wish I could do that. As a young man, did you have a good work ethic?

Brown

You know what, that's one of the things that I think I got from my grandmother. When I was in school every summer I used to work. One summer I worked for the city as a custodian. Whenever I worked nobody had to tell me what to do after I was finished with something. As I custodian, I knew there was something else that needed to be cleaned. Nobody had to come to me and say, "Clean this." I knew if it was dirty I needed to clean it.

Wright

You'd almost think it was a no-brainer wouldn't you?

Brown

Yeah, you know. Some things are a no-brainer, but I got my work ethic from my grandmother. Whatever I do, I just put myself into it. I always leave a good name wherever I work at.

Wright

What was your first work experience after high school?

Brown

David, this one is tough. All through school I was a slow learner. So, after high school the vocational school got me hooked up in this program and every time I think about it I have trouble talking about it. I was making $2.80 an hour in the summer of '85. Everybody that I worked around had physical disabilities, but I was labeled as having a learning disability. But I don't care what you say I had, $2.80 was still $2.80—I never forgot that.

Wright

It's almost demeaning isn't it?

Brown

Yes. It was probably my most demeaning time as a young man, and I think it is a sort of a springboard, just a push forward from wherever I was at that time.

Wright

Were you working for the hospital then?

Brown

No. I was able to get a summer job with the V.A. Hospital. I was working in stock and supply and after that position ran out I started working at Highsmith Rainey Hospital as a utility person, which means that I did three things on a regular basis. I washed pots and pans. I was in the dish room when people finished eating I was the one they'd bring their tray to. Other than that, I did stock and supply for Highsmith Rainey Hospital. I was there in '88 and I was with them for eight years. Working at Highsmith Rainey Hospital in the beginning my supervisor told me, "Dwight, I don't think you're going to work out." For some odd reason, I've always been the type of person that when you tell me something negative it's a motivating factor for me. So, as he shared with me, "Dwight, I don't think you're going to be here long," in my mind it came up, "He's going to like me and I'm going to be here for a long time."

Wright

I'd say eight years was a long time.

Brown

Yes. He was the supply supervisor and the way it ended up is on Tuesday and Friday he didn't want anyone else working with him but me. If I wasn't on the schedule he wanted me on the schedule.

Wright

Dwight, I've known you for years. It would be difficult for me to guess now that you had learning disabilities as a child. Where did you learn your excellent people skills?

Brown

I think I would have to pay that tribute to getting into sales. Getting into sales and also being involved in the community at a very early age. In my mid 20s, I was involved in a lot of community programs. I was a member of a group called 25 Black Men of Fayetteville and we as young black men thought that it was our position to look after and help the young ones so that they wouldn't go astray. We were like a mentor group. Other than that, during the same time I was doing the Cumberland County Minority Aids Speaker's Bureau. I was involved in so many things at the hospital and I was on the Hospital Activity Committee.

I was also on the Employee Council. What the Employee Council was, was each area in the hospital, like supervisors had somebody representing supervisors, cooks had somebody representing cooks, tray line people had somebody representing tray line people, and I represented the utility people. So, I think from me being involved in so many different group efforts and also initiating myself into sales has helped define my people skills. See, once I got into sales I never looked back. I was like a racehorse that pinned the ears back and just went for what I knew. Ain't no looking back now.

Wright

Tell us about your contribution to The Fayetteville Press Newspaper.

Brown

I came on board with The Fayetteville Press Newspaper in February of 1995. I never forgot that time or day. That was my second full-time sales position. Beyond that, I had never worked for a newspaper or media advertisement. I came in and J.J. Jones, the publisher, showed me around the paper and went over the advertisement sizes and the prices. From that point, I went out to every business that I possibly could. So, in a few months I ended up doubling my sales. I doubled my sales again a few months after that. A few more months later the publisher mentioned to me that he wanted me to be the sales manager. At that point in time, I was the sales manager somewhere within a year period and I was responsible for interviewing new account executives and I also put together a training program just for them. I did that primarily by whatever they brought to the table as an individual. So, I would change it on an individual basis. Some people I would spend more time with, some people less. But all of the training I did with them was in-house. I never went out with them to a business.

Wright

That's pretty good coming from a slow learner to a trainer. Let me ask you a tough question, Dwight. How did the label of slow learner affect you and how did you remove this stigma?

Brown

Well, it affected me. The biggest part is, you find yourself taking a longer period of time to learn one thing. When I decided that I was sick and tired of not being a regular and normal Joe, I was fed up. I looked at all the years I was out of high school and it was time for me to grow and develop. I didn't care at that point what label I had. The first thing I had to do was to dedicate my life to relearning. All I knew was that I didn't know, but I wanted to find out. The second thing and the next greatest thing that I ever did was I changed my friends. I started having criteria for my friends because I went from a point of deciding to let go of this stigma and grow as an individual and I wanted to learn constantly. If you were going to be my friend, you needed to know more than I knew or we couldn't be friends. So, I wanted my friends to be professional people, people who had knowledge and understanding—people who were on certain economic levels that I wasn't on. That, other than me relearning, was my objective. I dedicated my life to those two things in order to constantly build my Rolodex and build my relationship with people. I wanted to become a people magnet.

Wright

Tell us the best thing you've learned to this point.

Brown

David, this was the best one on the whole journey. The greatest thing that I've learned is that I, Dwight Brown, did not need anybody to validate me. I need to validate myself. I do not need anybody's approval for being successful. I don't need anybody to tell me yes or no. It's up to me. So, the last major thing that I had to learn was that I had to validate my own self, my own self-conviction. If I thought it in my mind that I had such an idea, I didn't need to share that with anyone else because it came up in my mind.

Wright

Tell us about the second greatest thing you've learned.

Brown

Now, that one is simple. The second greatest thing that I learned, which was one of the last ones, was learning about money and finances. I mean, really learning about money and finances. My grandmother was and is the greatest teacher that I have learned from. See, in my travels, I've learned from great businessmen and women from all around the country, but when it gets to this factor right here about money, my grandmother did not have a lot of schooling. She owned her own home in less than 10 years and she paid cash for her Lexus...

Wright

My goodness!

Brown

...In less than four years.

Wright

Goodness gracious.

Brown

I learned from her is that she hates payments and she despises credit cards.

Wright

Those are two of this culture's favorite things. It sounds like your grandmother is brilliant.

Brown

I owe her a lot of honor and gratitude.

Wright

Dwight, what has been your greatest impact on those people who are around you?

Brown

I give from my heart in whatever I do. I give from my heart. Let me share that in different ways. Anytime that I speak to a group, I speak through my heart and then through my head. Some people speak through their head and then come through their heart. I start out through my heart because I know all of the struggles I've been through and I want to share with each individual how important this thing is called growth and getting better. It's a life commitment to me. My other commitment is helping people. Some people look to get their college degree, but that degree doesn't help you to become a better person. You have to help yourself become a better person.

Wright

What do you want your legacy to be, Dwight?

Brown

That when anyone met Dwight he was the most caring person that they knew and he also wanted to help.

Wright

That would be a great mission statement for all of us. Dwight, I really appreciate you taking part in our program and especially in our book, *Conversations on Success*. I want to thank you for the time that you've spent with me here today. I've learned a lot about you and I've learned a lot about what you think. I think that our readers will really enjoy your life story starting out as a "slow learner" and I put quotation marks around slow learner in your case because I have seen you in action and you are an exemplary person. I really enjoyed the times that we have had together.

Brown

Me too.

Wright

Today we've been talking to Dwight Brown. He has experience as a motivational speaker, having delivered hundreds of speeches to groups all over the country. As we have learned, he is heavily involved in almost everything he has done; now he does a lot of community work with people who are disadvantaged as well as those who are not. We really appreciate this time today. Thank you so much.

Brown

Thank you, David.

About The Author

Dwight Brown has immeasurable experience as a motivational speaker having delivered speeches to approximately 300 groups. He is heavily involved with the Maranatha House and served as vice-president and eventually as the president of the Board of Directors, in which he is still a member of. He has helped shape the overall image and mold the vision of the organization. As a public speaker, Dwight is also a part of the highly coveted International Speakers Network. Dwight also has an extensive sales background and he thoroughly enjoys getting out developing new business contacts He has volunteered throughout Fayetteville and surrounding communities. His past involvement include: Cumberland County Minority Aids Speakers Bureau, Fuller School Adult Disabilities, Cumberland County Sheltered Workshop, and the Self Improvement Academy demonstrating Dwight's strong community connection.

Dwight Brown
The Fayetteville Press Newspaper
Phone: 910.323.3120
Brown Management Group
Phone: 910.491.4017
Fax: 910.323.1113
Email: fayepress@aol.com

Chapter 17

JIM KOUZES

THE INTERVIEW

David E. Wright (Wright)

Today we are talking to Jim Kouzes, a popular seminar and conference speaker. He shares his insights about the leadership practices that contribute to high performance in individuals and organizations. He leaves his audiences with practical leadership tools and tips that they can apply at work, at home, and in their communities. Jim is Chairman Americus of the Tom Peters Company, a professional services firm that specializes in leadership development. He is also an executive fellow in the Center for Innovation and Entrepreneurship, Leavey School of Business, Santa Clara University. Jim is the co-author of the award winning book, *The Leadership Challenge*, which is now in its third edition with over one million copies sold. *The Leadership Challenge*, available in eleven languages was a selection of the McMillan Executive Book Club and the Fortune Book Club. It's the winner of the James A. Hamilton Hospital Administrators' Book Award and Critics Choice Award. Jim also co-authored *Credibility: How Leaders Gain and Lose It: Why People Demand it,* which was chosen by Industry Week as one of the ten best management books of the year as well as *Encouraging The Heart, The Leadership Journal,*

The Leadership Challenge Workbook, and *The Leadership Practices Inventory.* Mr. Kouzes, welcome to *Conversations On Success.*

Jim Kouzes (Kouzes)

Thank you, David. It's a pleasure to be here.

Wright

Jim, today we're talking about success. In 2001, the International Management Council honored you with the prestigious Wilbur M. McFeely award. Past recipients include Peter Drucker, Lee Iacocca, Tom Peters, Ken Blanchard, Norman Vincent Peale, and Stephen Covey. Some would argue that this kind of recognition by ones peers denotes success more than money or position. What do you think?

Kouzes

David, the award, the McFeely Award, was a recognition that went to both Barry Posner and myself for our body of work. This began with *Leadership Challenge* and has continued in a collaboration that's lasted 20 years. That's far longer than many marriages. Any success that I may have achieved is a result of being blessed with a wonderful family, generous and supportive friends, and a great deal of luck. I can't claim self-credit for my accomplishments. You know I had the honor of interviewing Don Bennett who was the first amputee ever to climb Mt. Rainier, that's 14,410 feet, on one leg and two crutches. I asked him to tell me what the most important lesson was that he learned on that historic climb. He replied, "You can't do it alone." That message has always stuck with me. Not a day goes by when I don't think about that. It also keeps me humble and grateful. It's indeed an honor to be included with that esteemed company. Knowing that others appreciate our work and believe we've made a contribution to the field is affirming and very sustaining. It helps me get up in the morning.

Wright

I can imagine!

Kouzes

Yeah, it will last a lifetime. Money and position or momentary fame are very fleeting in its emerald. The real gift is the gift that others give to you of their own recognition for your contribution. I am very grateful. You're absolutely right in that recognition of peers is more important than anything.

Wright

You are acknowledged as an expert on leadership. Do you have a working definition of success that you apply to yourself and to others?

Kouzes

I have learned so much from the leaders that I've interviewed. This question reminds me of an interview I had with Major General John Stanford. He had set up the Military Traffic Command for the U.S. Army and then went on to be County Administrator, Fulton County, Georgia, and then on to become Superintendent of Schools in Seattle School District before he passed away. I asked him the question of how do you develop leaders for the future. He answered, "When anyone asks me that question, I tell them I have the secret to success in life." Your question reminded me of John's response. He said, "The secret to success is: Stay in love. Staying in love gives you the fire to really ignite other people, to see inside other people, to get more things done than other people. A person who is not in love doesn't really feel the kind of excitement that helps him to get ahead and to lead others to achieve. I don't know any other fire or anything in life that is more exhilarating and powerful a feeling than love is." Now, Wow! Huh? So, I can tell you I didn't expect to hear that from the Major General of the United States Army. But, in thinking about all the people that we've interviewed, John among them and many others, that response makes complete sense to me. Success is defined by how I feel, not what I possess.

Wright

Will you tell our readers a little bit about how you got started in business, and why you continue to do what you do?

Kouzes

I think it was the summer of 1969, David. I had just returned to the U.S. from Turkey where I had served in the Peace Corps for two years. I was 24 years old, and I was looking for a job. I still wanted to make a difference in the world. When I came back I was fortunate enough to be able to find a job in Austin, Texas, where I had fallen in love with Donna Burns who later became my wife for 30 years until her passing in 2000. I found a job working for Community Action

Program Training Institute where we travel around and do trainings for people in management, leadership, communications, and interpersonal skills, who had been working in the war on poverty effort. That led me to become involved with people from various organizations involved in the applied behavioral sciences, the people who did tea groups and sensitivity training and cross cultural training, which then lead to work at University of Texas, San Jose State University, and then finally Santa Clara University where I ended up meeting Barry. So, while the path took me in some respects around the world and to various states in the U.S., there was one clear common theme throughout everything which was training and development to help people learn better how to manage, lead, and work with others in teams. So, my collaboration with Barry was really a continuation of that, but it's been the most productive period of my life since getting together with him.

Wright

Your client list reads like a "Who's Who" in business and industry: AT&T, Bowing, Charles Schwab, Federal Express, and Dell Computer just to name a few of them. Your success must drive their motivation to use their services. What do you think organizations look for as they contact experts to help them?

Kouzes

David, in our research we found that credibility is the foundation of leadership. What my clients and my colleagues' clients look for is very akin to the same thing they look for in leaders, which is personal credibility. David, I think they are asking themselves, "Does he know what he's talking about? Does he have the expertise? Does he have the evidence to support it? Does he have the relevant experience? Can I trust him with the health and success of my business? Does he have my business interests at heart or is he in it for himself? Does he show up on time? Does he deliver what he promises? Does he say no when he can't deliver? Does he have the energy to see us through there?" They are asking themselves all those questions, but what that adds up to in one word is credibility. I really firmly believe, David, that what all professionals have to offer their clients is very simply their personal credibility, the most important personal asset I have, and I'll protect it with every fiber in my being.

Wright

The Wall Street Journal has cited you as one of the twelve most requested non-university executive education providers to United States companies. Could this be one of the keys to your success, the ability to take the message directly to the people who need it in a place convenient to them?

Kouzes

Very early on in my career, David, I was blessed with the opportunity to work with some of the most seasoned professionals in the business. One of the things I learned early on from a guy named Fred Margolis, who was a master trainer, was how learning takes place. I remember having lunch with Fred at an Italian Restaurant in Washington, D.C. He said to me, "Jim, what's the best way to learn something?" I always remember this scene. I thought I knew the answer because I'd been to a lot of experiential training. I said, "Well, the best way to learn something is to experience it yourself." I was very convinced that that was the right answer. He said, "No, the best way to learn something is to teach it to somebody else." I said, "Wow!" You know there are moments when you are asked to give a speech, David, or you're asked to teach your kids, or you're asked to lead a team of people and help acquaint them with a new software program or with a new procedure. Those are times when you know you really have to prepare yourself. You have to think, how am I going to transfer what I learned to somebody else? We all have experienced that, and Fred was very astute in saying, "Yes, it's about experience. We all have to go through it ourselves. But when you also are going to have to transfer that lesson to somebody else, that's when you really learn the best. We learn the best when we teach someone else." What I've tried to do is shape my style of training and development and of speaking. Even when I give a lecture, I'll always engage the audience, and I always ask them questions because I know that from their experience they have the answers. That is in fact how we did our research. We asked people to tell us their stories. So, the richness in this lesson of we learn best when we teach someone else has influenced everything I do. I think the best teachers and learners are master storytellers. That's very much what I think people want. Every time I give a talk, people say, "Well, give me an example of this. Give me an example of that. How does this apply in my situation?" So, while people want data, they want the evidence that what you are saying works, because in business you want evidence. You want something that works. They also want to know the stories and the examples.

Wright

Well, I've never thought of it that way before. I've always thought right off the top of my head that experiential learning would be the greatest of all learning models, but as I reflect on my life, you are absolutely true, or what he said was absolutely true.

Kouzes

Well, thank you. As you see it's very interesting. It was one of the epiphanious moments.

Wright

I'm fascinated by the amount of research you did in your book, *Leadership Challenge*. While talking to leaders all over the United States, did you get a sense that leaders are successful, or is leadership and success two entirely different subjects?

Kouzes

Originally my colleague and co-author, Barry Posner, along with Willis Brown corroborated on a research project done both in the U.S. and Canada. They looked at learning and leading. They found that those executives, who were more actively engaged in learning, are rated by others as more effective leaders. So, there's a positive correlation to learning and leading. The other important thing about that study is that they also found that it didn't matter what your learning style was. What mattered is that you use more of whatever your style was. In response to your question, I think that the message is very clear. You keep on learning throughout your life if you want to succeed. It's the learning that really comes first, and then everything else will follow.

Wright

Without using CEOs, well-known leaders or people of wealth, could you help our readers understand how the average Joe Homemaker, the student, attains success as they discharge their commitments and live their lives that are not in the spotlight?

Kouzes

Well, David, one of the things Barry and I decided early on was not to study CEOs. I know a whole bunch of them, and I have a great deal of respect for them. But we felt early on that it was important to study people in the middle and on the front lines. There is this myth in our society that success and power and importance is associated with position. If you are on the top, you're a success. So, everybody strives to be Chief Executive Officer. Everybody strives to be on the cover of Fortune Magazine. Everybody strives to be the number one guy or gal in the organization. You know, it's just been us! I don't think that success and being on top, being in the spotlight, is really one in the same thing. I have been known to look straight in the eyes of a Chief Executive Officer sitting in the audience and say, "With all due respect, you are not the most important person in this room." The audience often gasps at that, you know, "God, this guy just insulted my Chief Executive Officer!" Of course, I've told them ahead of time or her ahead of time, that I'm going to do this because we need to make this point. And normally the CEO will nod and agree with me. Then I will say, "The most important person in this room right now is each and every one of you. And to the members of your team you are the most important leader in this organization. It's you, not the Chief Executive Officer, who has the most impact on your day today performance." And, David, it is absolutely true that the research clearly indicates that the most important person in any relationship is that most immediate supervisor, if it's an organization. So, if it's in a family, whomever it might be, your mother or your father. If it's on a project team, it's the team leader. We, each and every one of us, can make a difference because we have an impact on those closest to us. So, there is really no difference in the behavior between a Chief Executive Officer and a front line employee, or even a parent when it comes to leadership. It's all the same behavior.

Wright

Jim, as a Boy Scout, you were chosen to participate in the inauguration of John F. Kennedy. Later you worked two years in the Peace Corps. Somewhere in the definition of success must be a charge to give back to the community or to the world some of what you have received. Is that true? If so, how do you suggest worthwhile projects to others?

Kouzes

I think, David, you are right. There comes a time in our lives, and it's often in the later years of our lives, halftime as Bob Buford has noted, when we feel the need to go from success to significance, when we move from thinking about material things to wanting to leave a legacy and make a contribution. I was very fortunate and very blessed to grow up in a family where early on in my life my mother was very active in the United Nations Association in our church. So, was my father. He was a civil servant and he took that role very seriously. When I joined the Peace Corps, I was involved in social services for 12 years. I think there is nothing more honorable, in my opinion, than serving others. Max Dupree, the former Chief Executive Officer of Harmon Miller once said that the first job as a leader was to define reality. The last was to say thank you. In between, it was to be a servant and a debtor. I found this to be a very profound statement and one that can only come from someone with a caring heart. God has given us a chance in this life to receive or to give. I learned early on that it is better to give than to receive. But you know what? When you give, you also get more back in your life so many times fold what you give. I think the kinds of projects I would recommend that people engage in are those that come from their hearts. Whether its your community, the environment, church, some political change you want to make that has to do with social justice, serving the poor and the needy, doing something for your kids, or your school or whatever is in your heart. At the end of the day, you'll sleep a lot better knowing that you have provided a service to someone else.

Wright

You know success is so allusive for some. I've known many people who have had great ideas, but just never seemed to get things going. Is there a formula that will make success more reachable, or is most success simply a function of being in the right place at the right time?

Kouzes

I'd say I'd feel might lucky in my life and I could never have planned my life the way it's turned out. I think that the whole notion of career planning is that to me it is a foreign concept. I couldn't have planned to run into Barry Posner, and then find out that we had a common interest, and planned to write half a dozen or actually 10 books together now, you know. I mean, that wasn't in the plan anywhere. It was serendipity which by way is from a book by Horrace

Walpole entitled and reprinted as *Serendip*. It was simply by combination of sarcasity and love that we were able to succeed. I think the common thread in my life and in the life of others who have been so fortunate is that I followed my calling. Luck comes to those who follow their calling. Success comes to those who follow their heart. Yet when I was giving a talk to a group of educators in university level, college level educators, a few weeks ago, and I asked them, "How many of you have been involved in career planning with your students?" and a lot of them raised their hands. Then I said, "Well, how many of you have talked to them about their calling?" Nobody raised his hand. So, we engage in this conversation with young people and with ourselves about how we can plan our careers but we never really think deeply about our true calling. A theologian and novelist once commented, I'm paraphrasing here, but I think he said something to the effect that you find your great call where your great joy meets the world's great need. I think that comes as close to a formula for success as I can find. Watch your great joy. Watch the great need in the world that enables you to use your great joy and therein lies your calling.

Wright

What are some of the projects that you have planned for yourself for the future to insure you happiness and success?

Kouzes

Well, I'm just finishing up I think it's our 10th book together. This one is an edited volume that is written. It's called *Christian Collections on Leadership Challenge.* We had five other colleagues who are Christian leaders reflect on each of our five practices, and we wrote the beginning and the closing to that. We are doing more work now with secondary schools and there'll probably be another book project come out of educational leadership. Of course, I'm continuing to do my own work in speaking with clients and doing consulting and training around leadership. One thing I have to say, David, is that leadership is my calling, and I'm going to stick with that for the remainder of my career. I'm not going to try to change jobs or change my profession. That I have I'll stay with. But I have picked up golf. I learned golf late in life after my wife passed away. It's a wonderfully humbling game. It also helps me to engage in a personal challenge and see if I can still learn to do anything new. But those are some of the projects I've got planned for myself. Barry and I are also sitting down and outlining a new book, which will be related more to leadership as personal, some of the personal sides of leadership that we've learned over the years that are so important.

Wright

I've got a theory after playing for many, many years that if you could find a hundred people who had scarred wrists from trying to slice them, 98 of them would be golfers. It is a humbling game, isn't it?

Kouzes

Yeah, well after watching the British Open and seeing some of the best golfers in the world end up with scores over par because the course was so difficult, then a guy who's never won a major before or any tournament before competing in his first major win it, it's a pretty amazing feat. In that is there is hope for all of us.

Wright

That's right.

Kouzes

It's also a great lesson in that just because you are one of the best golfers in the world doesn't mean you'll win every weekend. You know one of the things I love about learning this game is that it is a personal challenge. I was never one who was fond of sports metaphors. It just seemed to me that if you weren't active, you probably couldn't relate. But now that I've engaged in this, I'm finding all kinds of relevance to it. It's a wonderful game that for me is helping me to stay active and also learn something new. But that's my leisure and pleasure activity thing now.

Wright

Do you have any thoughts that might lead our readers to discover ways in which they might reach for more success in their businesses as well as their personal lives?

Kouzes

I'm of the belief that we actually don't reach for success. Success is not a thing out there that you can actually grab onto. It's not really a destination. It's a path that you travel down. You'll know you're on the right path if you keep finding joy along the way. If you keep leading people you can really call your friends, if you keep hearing your inner voice urging you to continue forward, if you find yourself constantly in awe and in wonder at all the opportunities for learning and growth. I think if you get all those messages daily, then you're on the path to success and your destination may never arrive, but you'll always know that you're on the right path.

Wright

Very interesting. Well, what an interesting conversation on leadership, Jim, and I really appreciate the time you have taken with me today. I know how busy your schedule is, and I really appreciate you taking this time.

Kouzes

It's always a lot of fun, David. Thank you very much. I appreciate it and stay in love.

Wright

I will. Today we have been talking to Jim Kouzes, who is a popular author and seminar and conference speaker. He teaches people how to increase their individual performance as well as we have found out today a lot of other things. Thank you so much, Jim, for being with us.

Kouzes

It's my pleasure, David, thank you for the opportunity.

About The Author

Jim is a highly-regarded leadership scholar and experienced executive, *The Wall Street Journal* has cited him as one of the twelve most requested non-university executive-education providers to U.S. companies. Jim is the Chairman Emeritus of Tom Peters Company, a professional service firm that specializes in developing leaders at all levels. He is also an Executive Fellow at the Center for Innovations and Entrepreneurship at Santa Clara University's Leavey School of Business.

Jim Kouzes
1784 Patio Drive
San Jose, California 95125
Phone: 877.866.9691 Ext. 239
Email: jim@kouzesposner.com
Website: www.leadershipchallenge.com